Suspensions

Wladimir Velminski

Suspensions

Control Processes in Eastern Europe from Iconoclasm to Cybernetics

Translated by Patrick Hubenthal

PETER LANG

Bibliographic Information published by the Deutsche Nationalbibliothek
The Deutsche Nationalbibliothek lists this publication in the Deutsche Nationalbibliografie; detailed bibliographic data is available in the internet at http://dnb.d-nb.de.

This publication funded by MECS Institut for Advanced Study on Media Cultures of Computer Simulation, Leuphana University Lüneburg (German Research Foundation Project KFOR 1927)

Umschlagabbildung: Ivan Razumov, Die Oktobernymphe, 2005.

Cover Design: © Olaf Gloeckler, Atelier Platen, Friedberg

Gedruckt auf alterungsbeständigem, säurefreiem Papier.
Druck und Bindung: CPI books GmbH, Leck

ISBN 978-3-631-67550-2 (Print)
E-ISBN 978-3-653-07085-9 (E-PDF)
E-ISBN 978-3-631-77485-4 (EPUB)
E-ISBN 978-3-631-77486-1 (MOBI)
DOI 10.3726/978-3-653-07085-9

Peter Lang – Berlin · Bern · Bruxelles · New York · Oxford · Wien · Warszawa

www.peterlang.com

This publication funded by MECS Institut for Advanced Study on Media Cultures of Computer Simulation, Leuphana University Lüneburg
(German Research Foundation Project KFOR 1927)

1 Entries for *suspension*

suspension, *n.* [1]

1. the act of suspending.
2. the state of being suspended.
3. temporary abrogation or withholding, as of a law, privilege, decision, belief, etc.
4. stoppage of payment of debts or claims because of financial inability or insolvency.
5. *Chem.* a. the state in which the particles of a substance are mixed with a fluid but are undissolved. b. a substance in such a state.
6. *Physical Chem.* a system consisting of small particles kept dispersed by agitation (mechanical suspension) or by the molecular motion in the surrounding medium (colloidal suspension).
7. something on or by which something else is suspended or hung.
8. something that is suspended or hung.
9. Also called suspension system. the arrangement of springs, shock absorbers, hangers, etc., in an automobile, railway car, etc., connecting the wheel-suspension units or axles to the chassis frame.
10. *Elect.* a wire, filament, or group of wires by which the conducting part of an instrument or device is suspended.
11. *Music.* a. the prolongation of a tone in one chord into the following chord, usually producing a temporary dissonance. b. the tone so prolonged.
12. *Rhet.* the heightening of interest by delay of the main subject or clause, especially by means of a series of parallel preceding elements.

Fig. 1

2 Iconoclastic impulses

2.1 Black spots

On the eve of the October Revolution, the Russian prince Evgeny Trubetskoy announced "one of the greatest and most paradoxical events in the recent history of Russian culture" – the "unveiling of the icon before our very eyes." He felt "compelled to speak now of this unveiling," as he wrote, because up to that point "everything about the icon had been hidden from our view – lines, colors, and especially the *spiritual meaning* of this thing that is unique in the world of art. And in fact, it is precisely this meaning that keeps our Russian epic alive."[1]

Prince Trubetskoy's "unveiling of the icon" followed discussions that were in vogue in Russia in the early twentieth century. In 1904, the icon collection of the businessman and art patron Pavel Tretyakov, which had been donated to the city of Moscow before his death in 1898, was shown at the gallery bearing his name (Fig. 1). This exhibition of the fruits of Old Russian icon painting, which until then had been preserved primarily in churches, was enthusiastically received by a public that included foreign visitors such as Henri Matisse, who was shown the works when he visited Russia in 1911, and who saw in them "the primary source of all artistic endeavour,"[2] from which all modern artists were obliged to draw.

Intensive study of these historical cultural treasures resulted in another big exhibition in 1913, this time at the Institute of Archaeology in Moscow. In their fascination with icons, the unveilers cared little for the fact that the sacral significance of these religious images, whose primary purpose had been to inspire awe in their viewers, was completely eclipsed by their aesthetic potential and resulting profanation. These profaned sacred images were credited with a new "impossibility of using," which had "its emblematic place in the Museum."[3] According to Pavel Muratov, the exhibition's curator, its primary function was the presentation of the unknown: "Many, perhaps all, were surprised by the exhibition. There before us stood unveiled a new artistic movement – stood unveiled a whole new art. It seemed hardly imaginable that no one in the West had ever seen these strong and gentle colors, these artful lines and soulful countenances."[4]

To Prince Trubetskoy, it was obvious why this "Russian treasure"[5] had been overlooked:

> We walked by the icon, but we did not see it. It seemed nothing more than a black spot in the center of the golden oklad; we knew it only as such. And then suddenly – a complete transvaluation of values. The gold or silver riza enclosing the icon is exposed as a relatively late invention from the end of the sixteenth century; it is, above all, the creation of a pious tastelessness betraying a loss of religious and artistic meaning. In essence, we are faced here with an unconscious iconoclasm ... in the approach not only to aesthetics, but also – and especially – to religion. And the more expensive and ornate an oklad is, the more clearly it illustrates the abyss of everyday dullness that has built this golden partition between us and the icon.[6]

Neat as Trubetskoy's description of the icon as a "black spot" and his reference to "unconscious iconoclasm" may be, his characterization requires a few clarifications and historical amplifications. When

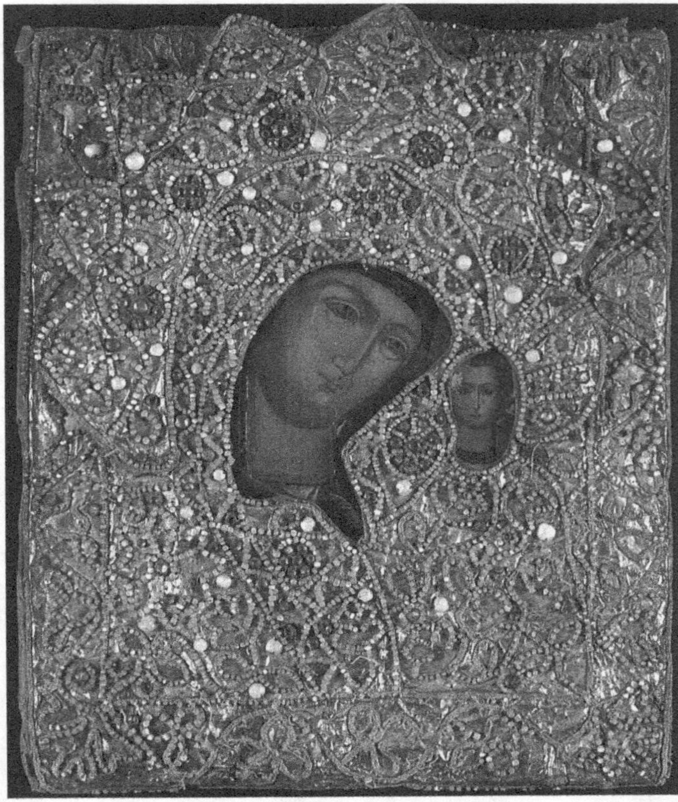

Fig. 2

the prince speaks of a "golden partition" inserted between viewer and icon, he is equating two different terms, sometimes speaking of an "oklad" and sometimes of a "riza." The difference between the two becomes clear when we focus on the size of the "black spot." To the prince, this was not an allusion to Malevich's *Black Square*, but rather an attempt to illuminate the condition of the icons still visible within their housings. Whereas the covering known as a riza merely encloses the outline of the saint's figure (Fig. 2), the oklad

Fig. 3

conceals everything but the faces, hands, and feet beneath itself (Fig. 3).[7] The confusion of these terms is due to the fact that in Russian Orthodox terminology, the word *oklad* has come to denote any kind of decoration or ornamentation that may be added to an icon.

Trubetskoy's characterization of the oklad as a "relatively late invention from the end of the sixteenth century" is not quite accurate either. While the degree of decoration did increase during the Baroque era, there are also numerous references to oklads proving that they already existed in the age of Iconoclasm.[8]

History does not record whether the icon's golden sheath served as a sort of portable armor for sanctioned acts of war, when the sacred portraits were carried along at the front, or perhaps an aegis that lent the devotional image a healing tactility during processions; a shield that would protect the saint from the exposing gaze of the all too human or, conversely, bind the unpredictable potency emanating from the saint's image, as has been described in numerous accounts of miracles.[9] The brightness of the precious metals, especially the gold, evoked a direct association with the saint's aura, which helped make goldsmithing the foremost art form of the Middle Ages.[10] To avoid the possibility of creating an idol, the saints' faces and extremities were typically left uncovered by the costly materials of which the oklads were made.

The parallels between the oklad and the Ark of the Covenant, which was made of gilded acacia wood, led the patriarchs meeting at the Seventh Ecumenical Council in 787 to sanction the veneration of these sacred images painted on wood and covered in gold.[11] Following the iconoclast Synod of Hieria held in 754, this meeting, also known as the Second Council of Nicaea, famously decided in favor of the representation of the "figure of the sacred and life-giving Cross ... whether made in colours or mosaic or other materials ... placed suitably in the holy churches of God, on sacred vessels and vestments, on walls and pictures, in houses and by roads; that is to say, the images of our Lord God and Saviour Jesus Christ, of our immaculate Lady the holy Mother of God, of the honourable angels and all saints and holy men."[12]

This mandated iconoduly, as opposed to iconolatry, was accompanied by the emergence of quite substantial image coverings meant to shield the manifestation of the sacred from profane acts, and thus also to rein in the power of the numinous.[13] In Russia

Fig. 4

at the height of the Middle Ages, oklads were produced only for especially venerable icons believed to possess healing powers, which were regularly carried at the head of processions as a consequence (Fig. 4).

Oklads were made of gold or silver, depending on the financial resources available to the church authorities. The artisan charged with preparing the precious metal typically decorated the image's ritual garment with punchwork; the more precious and elaborate the oklad was supposed to look, the more varied the sheets of precious metal assembled to create the casing. To lend stability to the icon hammered into the oklad, and to achieve the desired "synthesis," seams and cracks were sealed with wax.

While the earliest oklads were quite simple (if made of precious metal), intended mainly to highlight the special characteristics of the icon, during the Renaissance they became increasingly ornamented – Trubetskoy's "abyss of everyday dullness." As tasteless as the prince may have felt the tradition to be, it is also linked to a fundamental element of religion: sacrifice.[14] In the Russian Orthodox tradition, in particular, sacrificial acts remain an important part of churchgoing to this day. Those wishing to make a offering approach the oklad-encased icon, bow, and make the sign of the cross three times. They then kiss the oklad and present their offering, an act that in those days typically consisted in affixing an ornament to the oklad. Only this sacrificial act "legitimizes the power of touch"[15] that allows those making the offering to make "contact" with its intended recipient and name their request. The act concludes with three more signs of the cross and another bow. It was this way of making offerings that overloaded the oklads with ornamentation – an outcome that displeased Peter the Great, who issued an edict in 1722 forbidding the adornment of oklads.[16]

"Where sacrifice ceases, so does religion."[17] Religion does not cease, however, when the sacrificial act is systematically transformed. Following Peter's decree, offerings were to be made by purchasing a candle and placing it in front of the sacred image.[18] But the ban on attaching objects to oklads did not prevent the icon housings from becoming more and more elaborate, especially after Peter's death. Gold and silver were joined by other materials such as enamel and gemstones, which were used to add halos and other decorative elements to the oklad. The result of such extraordinary and extravagant ornamentation was that only slits remained for the saints' faces and hands, or in some cases only their feet. As a result, icon painting stagnated, with the icons themselves becoming merely preliminary sketches, until eventually only the parts visible through the slits in the oklad were painted, while the rest of the wood was left untouched.[19]

Only the reductivism of the nineteenth century brought about a simplification of the oklad, for which no less a figure than the jeweler Peter Carl Fabergé was responsible, and which ensured that the oklad would remain a monumental presence in the churches. The ability to manufacture metal fittings by machine, together with the simplified painting of the oklad openings, gradually led to a migration of small oklad-covered icons into the humblest of households.[20] These so-called *fol'gushki*, or "tinfoil oklads," made from thin sheets of cheap metal, were hung in the most sacred place in the home, the highest corner of the room, where the face of the saint, seen from below, appeared as no more than a "black spot."

2.2 Black days

As mentioned above, Trubetskoy's outrage in 1916 knew no bounds: "What would we say if we saw Botticelli's or Raphael's Madonna clad in gold and glittering gemstones?! No less a crime has been committed against the great works of Old Russian icon painting; the time is not far off now when that will become clear to all of us."[21]

The prince's statements in this regard are not exceptional; they reflect the way the icon was generally viewed by the intelligentsia, a view that was widespread in 1910 and that ultimately led scholars of the icon to focus primarily on the theory of archetype and image.[22] The fundamental importance of the interplay of isolation and union between icon and oklad went unnoticed. Nor was there any recognition of the fact that the critical moment of tactile/visual contact with the icon was not necessarily precipitated by making an offering: the oklad, already clearly foregrounded, itself presented the opportunity for such contact, making it "visible" and thereby binding belief to the possibility of "comprehending."[23] Profanation took its course:

> Everything that has heretofore passed for an icon now falls apart before our eyes. The black spots are removed. In defiance of our native ignorance, the breach in even the most golden armor of the oklad is broken wide open. The icon's beauty has already been revealed to our eyes, yet we are still only halfway there. To us, the icon remains the object of a superficially aesthetic pleasure that fails to penetrate to its spiritual meaning. At the same time, we have already comprehended the true beauty of the icon's content in its lines and colors. These are beautiful, however, only as the translucent expression of that spiritual content that is embodied in them. Those who see only the outer surface of that content are not far removed from those who admire the gilded rizas and dark spots. For in the end, the phenomenon of the riza is merely the product of another form of superficial aestheticism.[24]

The oklad was now no longer an interactive mantle that placed the icon in a hierarchy, but rather a mere coating, an elaborate disruptive element, to be removed so that all possible manifestations of the sacred image could be understood:

> The unveiling of the icon thus remains incomplete. What is happening before our eyes ... is only the laying of the foundation. When this language of symbolic expression and form, which still remains unintelligible and obscure to us, has been deciphered, we will have to rewrite not just the history of Russian art, but the entire history of Old Russian culture. For here too, our gaze still remains tethered to the surface. ... The unveiling of the icon gives us the opportunity to look deep into the soul of the Russian people, and to hear the confession of the icon, given voice in glorious works of art.[25]

Fig. 5

Yet even that language is, as we know, a mute language requiring careful translation.[26] To the extent, then, that a deterioration of the aura can be posited with regard to the "unveiling of the icon," the cause is not only the icon's "technological reproducibility," but also the naïveté of the image-idolizers, who, in allowing themselves to be blinded by the icons' shapes and colors, sought to investigate the power of these religious images while ignoring their ritual function.

On one point, however, Prince Trubetskoy was right. "Everything that [had] passed for an icon" had indeed fallen apart. The dethronement of the tsar, the melting-down of the oklads, and the demolition of the churches were to follow.

2.3 Black square

The era of the "unveiling of the icon" also saw the "invention" of the Black Square by Kazimir Malevich, who conceptualized it as an icon of the new art: "This is the form of a new living organism. ... It is not painting; it is something else. I had the idea that were humanity to draw an image of the Divinity after its own image, perhaps the Black Square is the image of God as the essence of His perfection on a new path for today's fresh beginning."[27]

That painting, created in 1915, was shown in the groundbreaking *Last Futurist Exhibition 0,10 (Zero-Ten)*, where Malevich had it hung in the highest corner of the gallery – a location, as noted above, that was traditionally reserved for the Russian Orthodox icon (Fig. 5). The way Malevich characterized his image as being in a state of flux between icon and iconoclasm; the meaning he ascribed to the form of the square and the colors black and white; the intermedia comparisons to religious portraiture: all this has been the subject of meticulous scholarly review in recent years.[28] But while those investigations have scrutinized the artist's letters and other writings, some of which are quite cryptic, they have attached little importance to the opinions of his contemporaries. It is precisely in such accounts, however, that the impact of the first encounters with the icons of modernity can be read: "Without a number, but rather in the corner, directly below the ceiling, in the sacred place, hangs Mr. Malevich's "creation," a depiction of the Black Square in a white frame. No doubt this is the "icon" with which the Messrs. Futurists propose to replace Madonnas and immodest portraits of Venus."[29]

The author of these words, Alexandre Benois, was one of the most feared and renowned art critics of the day. The future head curator of the Hermitage Museum, he had reported on the great icon exhibitions years earlier and was now interested to see what the new artists had created from the "primary source of all artistic endeavour." He wrote: "The Black Square in a white oklad: this is no

Fig. 6

joke, no simple affront, no minor episode that happened to occur in the house on Marsovo Pole, but rather an act of self-assertion on the part of that beginning that bears the impudence of devastation in its very name, and that boasts of the way it is driving all of us – with the help of pride, good cheer, and disdain for all that is delicate and endearing – into the abyss."[30]

What concerns us here is not the danger the conservative art historian saw in Suprematism, but rather his description of the *Black Square* as an icon. In his reference to the *Black Square*'s "white oklad," Benois establishes a clear connection between the painting's white border and the icon's garb. And it is precisely in that seemingly insignificant garment that the operative quality of the image's power lies hidden, without which its potency can never be exhausted: "The forms in which religion is clothed are all unimportant, and yet it is with them that the act of religiousness is expressed, and the signs, taken by themselves, are symbols; in part, a sign itself is dissimilar to that which it symbolizes."[31]

Malevich made use of precisely that border, which remained affixed to Orthodox icons until the end of the nineteenth century

– and which was, with the "unveiling of the icon," subjected to intense criticism at the beginning of the twentieth – to emphasize a similarity to the still-unprofaned icon (Fig. 6), thus amplifying both the power of his own icon and the intensity of the sacred epiphany.

2.4 Black caviar

After the fall of the Soviet Union, the trajectory of belief shifted again in Russia, with commerce and Orthodoxy taking the place of monumental propaganda and ideological agitation. The ornate and richly decorated oklads returned to the churches, where once again they cover the images of the saints, for the church fathers have not forgotten that covering the sacred strengthens authority and invigorates faith. Yet the processions that are supposed to bring healing powers are also accompanied by phenomena such as trance and hysteria.

One such incident took place in Moscow in 2005. The New Tretyakov Gallery – an offshoot of the old gallery where the first icon exhibition had been held, and the same gallery that was now home to the *Black Square* – was hosting the exhibition *Russian Pop Art*, which centered on artists from the Sots Art movement. As one of the most prominent artists in that movement, Alexander Kosolapov could not possibly have been left out of the show. One of his signature pieces, *Lenin Coca-Cola* (1982), shows Lenin in profile next to the slogan "Coca-Cola. It's the real thing" and beneath that the name "Lenin," as though the message had come from the revolutionary leader himself.

Kosolapov has pursued such strategies of confrontational emphasis since the beginning of his artistic career. Although he did execute some commissions for socialist-realist work in the early 1970s, when he had just graduated from art school, at the same time he was also creating other pieces that lampooned the symbolic economy

Fig. 7

of his commissioned work. This artistic calculus was made plain in his 1974 painting *Aurora* (Fig. 7). The stark red outlines of the ship that rang in the revolution, painted on a sky-blue background, stand as an expression of Soviet pride: the *Aurora* in all her shimmering golden glory. Yet in the shimmering of the ship, another world lies hidden. On closer inspection, one notices signs of decay, peeling paint: underneath is another painting, which Kosolapov has said he found in the trash.[32] Like the "black spot" of an icon, the inside of the ship draws in the viewer's gaze, and the image of the vaunted warship is transformed into a romantic seascape. Thus disguised, socialist realism's ideological hierarchy of formal doctrines arrives

Fig. 8

at an almost sentimental creation of political unimpeachability and vanishes into it.

Going beyond the founding works of the movement, the 2005 exhibition was also supposed to feature more recent works from the postsocialist era, works created after the fall of the Soviet Union. Kosolapov had begun taking black-and-white photographs of black caviar in 1989. In allusion to the *Black Square*, he made 14-inch-square prints of these images, which he named *Ikra* (caviar) (Fig. 8).

This work, which of course evidenced not just allusions to Malevich, but also connections to Andy Warhol's critique of consumer society, went virtually unnoticed. When the artist decided,

Fig. 9

seven years later, to extend the piece by adding an oklad, he decided not to use a square oklad like the one that had enclosed the *Black Square*, instead choosing a metal frame with an opening whose shape, iconographically speaking, was of the *eleusa* type – that is, the Madonna with the Christ Child (Fig. 9). In his comments on this covering, Kosolapov – whose aim, let us recall, is to expose the mechanisms of the symbolic economy – frequently made reference to Warhol's statement that in America, the president and the "bum on the corner" both drink the same Coca-Cola.[33] Black caviar, on the other hand – which we associate with Russia – is available to every Russian president, but not to the everyday citizen. By surrounding caviar with an oklad, Kosolapov draws the viewer's eye to a critique of capitalism via the unattainability of a cult commodity. He holds a mirror up to Russian society and creates a new icon, the icon of his time.

When Kosolapov was invited to take part in the *Russian Pop Art* exhibition, he suggested that his *Caviar Icon* be included. The decision to hang it in the central room of the gallery reflected the curators' enthusiasm for the piece. Many reviews approved of this choice and applauded the sophistication of the exhibition's concept. According to the curator, Andrei Erofeev, critics saw Kosolapov's *Caviar Icon* as a masterpiece, the heart of the show.[34]

Not everyone shared this opinion, however. In the week after the opening, the director of the gallery received a letter of complaint, bearing fifty signatures, from an archimandrite in the Russian Orthodox Church. It read: "We hereby affirm that the object in question incites social and religious enmity and hostility in the authors of this letter."[35] The gallery's directors decided to take the picture down. The only thing Erofeev was able to do was to reproduce the outlines of the *Caviar Icon* on the white wall with a fat black marker, highlighting the empty space. In place of the oklad-framed image, a black outline drawn around a nail pointed to the censorship that had been brought to bear in response to the

Fig. 10

pressure from the church; at the same time, it also marked the power of absence.

The aura of elitism and authoritarianism associated with an expensive product like caviar, and also with the Orthodox Church, is further intensified in Kosolapov's newest piece, *Madonnas* (Fig. 10). Three naked young women pose behind three oklads; in front of each hangs a thurible. The women's erotic poses are unmistakable: with every feminine attribute they possess, they offer themselves to the viewer. The icon borders placed before them have been released from the duty of sacred preservation and take on the function of directing the gaze. The viewer becomes a voyeur; a fleeting glance is no longer possible. The icon borders now serve only the desire to gaze at the naked bodies that are offered up, an ideological frame for the "aesthetics of existence" being modeled.

Like a diffraction aperture, the oklad renders visible a wide array of interference patterns produced by the overlapping of political, religious, and aesthetic dynamics whose intensity depends on the viewer's perspective, and whose potential remains to be explored. One thing, however, is clear: without this aperture, without the oklad, these patterns would never have appeared.

3 Topographic reflections

3.1 Journeys through the mail

The movements of parcels and people are interwoven with the engineering of space. Before a postman delivers letters, a pedestrian disappears into a subway entrance, or Santa Claus comes sliding down the chimney, the particulars of every piece of information and every point along the way must be studied to ascertain their *dispositions*. Because no matter how long a subway ride or journey through the mail may be, it should be planned in such a way that every stop, every node, every junction will ideally be passed only once.

One such pattern presented a puzzle for the eighteenth-century residents of the city of Königsberg: how could one walk across all seven bridges over the River Pregel – which connected two islands with each other and with the mainland – without crossing any bridge more than once? The solution to this problem, given by the Swiss mathematician Leonhard Euler, laid the foundations of graph theory; its further development would create new topological patterns.

The letter containing the bridge puzzle was delivered to Euler in Saint Petersburg in March 1736. In it, Carl Leonhard Gottlieb Ehler, the mayor of Danzig (which was not far from Königsberg), and Heinrich Kühn, a professor of mathematics, present their request: "It would give me and our Mr. Kühn great pleasure, putting us greatly in your debt, most learned sir, if you would see fit to send us the solution, together with its proof, of a problem no doubt well known to you: that of the disposition of Königsberg's seven bridges. This is a task offering opportunities for numerous calculations and deserving of the attention of your genius. I have included a sketch."[1]

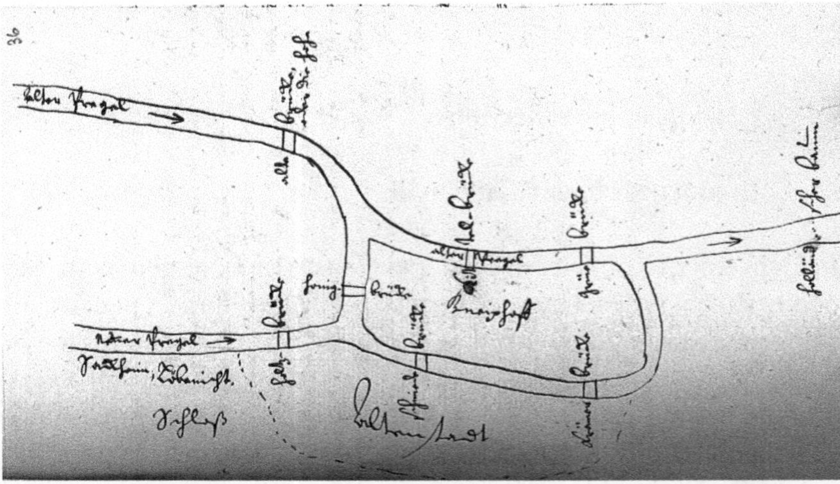

Fig. 11

Ehler's drawing includes all the essential details: the parts of the city, the islands and their names, the river and the direction of its flow, and of course the seven bridges: Grünebrücke, Köttelbrücke, Honigbrücke, Schmiedebrücke, Krämerbrücke, Hohebrücke, and Holzbrücke. In the letter, Ehler suggests that this problem could be assigned to the geometry of position (*geometria situs*), as propagated by Gottfried Wilhelm Leibniz and, more recently, Christian Wolff.

At first, Euler seems confused by the letter, since he is not familiar with the problems Leibniz and Wolff are supposed to have addressed. On the other hand, he is surprised that no one seems to have solved the problem of the Königsberg bridges yet: the problem, he writes, is very clear, and "the solution is based on pure argumentation, with no need to adduce any of the laws of mathematics."[2]

He nonetheless takes the assignment, and on March 13, 1736, he lays out the problem and its solution to the Italian mathematician Giovanni Jacobo Marinoni, with whom he has recently struck up a correspondence. Marinoni is working in a related field, dealing with questions of cartography and astronomy in Vienna at the same time Euler is creating maps of the Russian Empire and its cities in Saint Petersburg. Euler considers the statement of the Königsberg bridge problem "banal," but because the path to its solution does not belong "to geometry, nor to algebra, nor to the art of combinatorics," as he writes, it is a task worthy of his attention and "might belong to that *geometry of position* of which Leibniz spoke."[3]

Euler's experiment in notation begins with the encoding of Königsberg's bridges, which he operationalizes by labeling them with the lowercase letters *a*, *b*, *c*, *d*, *e*, *f*, and *g*.

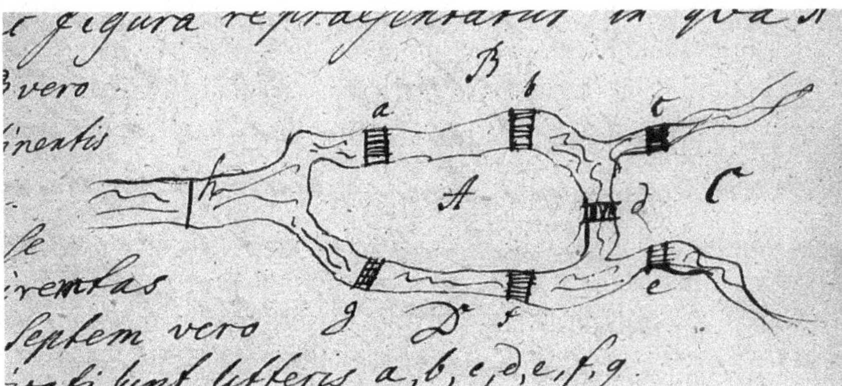

Fig. 12

The island of Kneiphof is given the capital letter *A*, while the river's other banks are labeled *B*, *C*, and *D*. The lengths of the bridges and the direction of the river's flow are of no consequence, in Euler's view, nor does he differentiate between island and mainland. The problem is not characterized by sizes or lengths, only by the algebraic code of the letters.

Now Euler begins to count: "First of all, we must determine how many areas are separated by water – those that have no connection to one another but by bridge. In our example, there are four such areas, *ABCD*. Next, we must determine whether the number of bridges leading to these areas is even or odd."[4] Königsberg's bridges are arranged in such a way that there are five leading to area *A* and three to each of the other areas. That is sufficient information for Euler to make the following statement of number theory:

> If the number of bridges leading to each separate area were even, then such a walk as we have been discussing would be possible, and one would also be able to start the walk in any area desired. Now, if two of these numbers were odd, which is also possible, the walk described would still be possible, but one would have to start in one of the two areas with an odd number of bridges. However, if there are more than two areas with an odd number of bridges leading to them, such a walk is not possible.[5]

This inherently logical and clear solution raises just one question: why does Euler label the parts of the city and the bridges with letters if he is only going to count them, instead of working with the algebraic codes?

3.2 A problem in cryptography

An explanation of Euler's indexical notation can be found in a rather didactically constructed essay published in 1736 in the journal of the Russian Academy of Sciences in Saint Petersburg. Euler appears to have pursued the ideas raised by the constructors of the puzzle (to whom he replied that same year[6]), since his essay, which promises “the solution of a problem relating to the geometry of position,” makes explicit reference to Leibniz: “In addition to that branch of geometry which is concerned with magnitudes, and which has always received the greatest attention, there is another branch, previously almost unknown, which Leibniz first mentioned, calling it the *geometry of position*. This branch is concerned only with the determination of position and its properties; it does not involve measurements, nor calculations made with them.”[7]

Euler describes the problem that had been brought to him, stating that he “had no doubt that it was concerned with the geometry of position – especially as its solution involved only position, and no calculation was of any use.”[8] His solution, he says, “is based on a quite convincing proof, with the aid of which one can immediately discover, for any similar problem, whether or not such a walk is possible over any number of bridges, regardless of their arrangement.”[9] Euler describes the technique he has invented to solve such problems as an “example of the geometry of position.” His “whole method,” he claims, “relies on the particularly convenient way in which the crossing of a bridge can be represented,” using the letters *A*, *B*, *C*, and *D* “for each of the land areas separated by the river.”[10]

After these semiotic steps (the same ones previously sent to Marinoni), Euler sets off on his graphematic travels:

> If a traveller goes from *A* to *B* over bridge *a* or *b*, I write this as *AB* – where the first letter refers to the area the traveller is leaving, and the second refers to the area he arrives at after crossing the bridge. Thus if the traveller leaves *B* and crosses into *D* over bridge *f*, this crossing is represented by *BD*, and the two crossings *AB* and *BD* combined I shall denote by the three letters *ABD*, where the middle letter *B* refers both to the area which is entered in the first crossing and to the one which is left in the second crossing.[11]

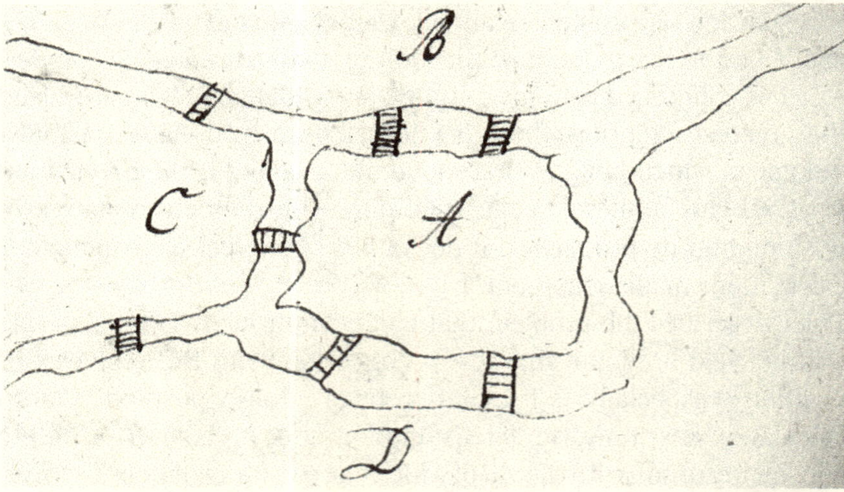

Fig. 13

As a result of this concatenation of indexical symbols, a walk over two bridges is indicated by three letters, a walk over three by four, a walk over four by five, "and in general, however many bridges the traveller crosses, his journey is denoted by a number of letters one greater than the number of bridges. Thus the crossing of seven bridges requires eight letters to represent it."[12]

The topographic description of the city has now literally turned into a media landscape[13] concerned not with lengths or curvatures, but only with the linking of letters. In the stipulated walk over Königsberg's seven bridges, the poetics of space must therefore generate a semiotic chain consisting of eight letters. The links of this chain must be "arranged so that the letters *A* and *B* are next to each other twice, since there are two bridges, *a* and *b*, connecting the areas *A* and *B*; similarly, *A* and *C* must be adjacent twice ... and the pairs *A* and *D*, *B* and *D*, and *C* and *D* must occur together once each."[14]

In cryptographic terms, what Euler is doing here is determining the absolute frequency of the letters within the series constituting the chain of letters that "spells" the traveler's journey across the bridges. "The problem," he writes, "is therefore reduced to finding a sequence of eight letters, formed from the four letters *A*, *B*, *C*, and *D*, in which the various pairs of letters occur the required number of times." This is the exact point at which Euler departs from the poetic code. Before he starts looking for a desired sequence of letters, he wants to know whether there is such a sequence to be found. He therefore needs to "find a rule which will be useful in this case, and in others, for determining whether or not such an arrangement can exist."[15]

3.3 Poetic walks

To better illustrate this number-theory game, Euler leaves Königsberg's constellation of bridges behind and sets out on new imaginary walks involving another river, a random number of bridges, and the areas *A* and *B*.

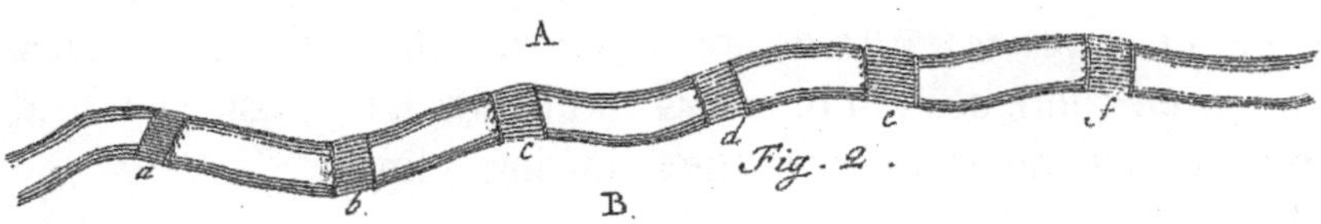

Fig. 14

> If a traveller crosses this bridge, he must either have been in *A* before crossing, or have come into *A* after crossing, so that in either case the letter *A* will occur once in the representation described above. If three bridges (*a*, *b*, and *c*, say) lead to *A*, and if the traveller crosses all three, then in the representation of his journey the letter A will occur twice, whether he starts his journey from *A* or not. Similarly, if five bridges lead to *A*,

> the representation of a journey across all of them would have three occurrences of the letter *A*.[16]

Euler's purpose in making this basic observation is to clearly show that the frequency of a capital letter depends on the number of bridges leading to it. And, as he is quick to note, that frequency also depends on whether the number of bridges in the area is even or odd. Where there is an odd number of bridges, Euler instructs us to increase the number by one and then divide it in half.

Having laid this cornerstone of graph theory and obtained the number that indicates how often the letter *A* appears in his imaginary city, Euler then turns his gaze back to Königsberg: "In a series of eight letters, representing the crossing of seven bridges, the letter *A* must occur three times, and the letters *B*, *C*, and D twice each – but this cannot happen in a sequence of eight letters. It follows that such a journey cannot be undertaken across the seven bridges of Königsberg"[17] (Fig. 13).

The impossibility of poetic strolls over the seven bridges of Königsberg generates a program. To be able to decide whether it is possible, in any given configuration of rivers and bridges, to cross each bridge exactly once, Euler proposes the following rule:

> I first denote by the letters *A*, *B*, *C*, etc. the various areas which are separated from one another by the water. I then take the total number of bridges, add one, and write the result above the working which follows. Thirdly, I write the letters *A*, *B*, *C*, etc. in a column, and write next to each one the number of bridges leading to it. Fourthly, I indicate with an asterisk those letters which have an even number next to them. Fifthly, next to each even one I write half the number, and next to each odd one I write half the number increased by one. Sixthly, I add together these last numbers, and if this

> sum is one less than, or equal to, the number written above, which is the number of bridges plus one, I conclude that the required journey is possible. It must be remembered that if the sum is one less than the number written above, then the journey must begin from one of the areas marked with an asterisk, and it must begin from an unmarked one if the sum is equal.[18]

Letters, numbers, and symbols are the semiotic practices that constitute the Eulerian poetics of space, a space the mathematician, spiderlike, goes on weaving. Now there are "two islands *A* and *B* surrounded by water which leads to four rivers." The correlate of Euler's imaginary city, meanwhile, is not the streets but rather fifteen imaginary bridges leading over imaginary water that surrounds imaginary islands. In this imaginary interconnected city, Euler asks the now familiar question of "whether one can arrange a journey which crosses each bridge exactly once."[19]

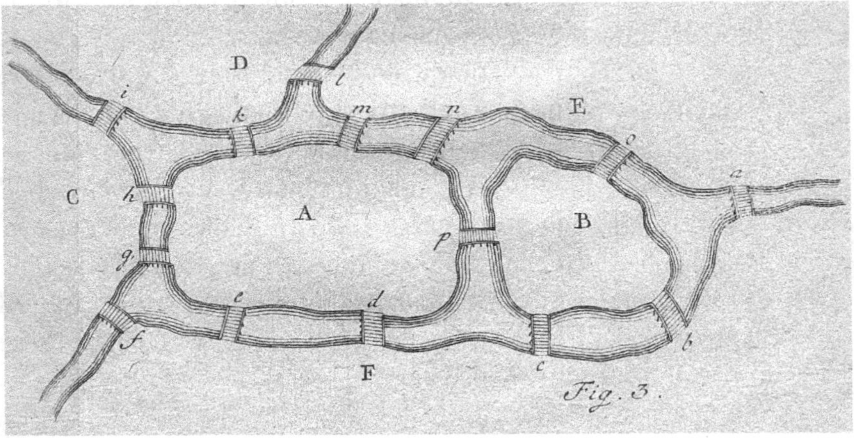

Fig. 15

Euler's poetics of space is made up of seven interweavings:

> First, therefore, I name all the areas separated by water as *A*, *B*, *C*, *D*, *E*, *F*, so that there are six of them. Next I increase the number of bridges (15) by one, and write the result (16) above the working which follows.
>
> | | | 16 |
> |---|---|---|
> | *A**, | 8 | 4 |
> | *B**, | 4 | 2 |
> | *C**, | 4 | 2 |
> | *D*, | 3 | 2 |
> | *E*, | 5 | 3 |
> | *F**, | 6 | 3 |
> | | | 16 |
>
> Thirdly, I write the letters *A*, *B*, *C*, etc. in a column, and write next to each one the number of bridges which lead to the corresponding area, so that eight bridges lead to *A*, four to *B*, and so on. Fourthly, I indicate with an asterisk those letters which have an even number next to them. Fifthly, I write in the third column half the even numbers in the second column, and then I add one to the odd numbers and write down half the result in each case. Sixthly, I add up all the numbers in the third column in turn, and I get the sum 16; since this is equal to the number (16) written above, it follows that the required journey can be made if it starts from area *D* or *E*, since these are not marked with an asterisk.[20]

In taking these seven mental walks, Euler lays down a poetic path through his imaginary city: *EaFbBcFdAeFfCgAhCiDkAmEnApBoElD*. [21]

Fig. 16

3.4 Imaginary cities

To make possible such an aesthetically pleasing walk in Königsberg, Euler had already suggested, in his letter to Marinoni, that another bridge be built at the point marked by *h* (Fig. 12). This would add asterisks to areas *B* and *D*, and "areas *A* and *C* would have an odd number of bridges."[22] According to Euler's seven rules, the walk should then start in area *A* or *C*.

Euler's proposal that an eighth bridge be built at the point indicated to solve the circuit problem is also the first example of an arrangement of space whose facets specifically paralleled the formation of topological knowledge.

In 1905, the city fathers of Königsberg implemented Euler's recommendation and built a stone bridge. Although this new bridge, the Kaiserbrücke (Fig. 16), was not constructed at the location Euler had recommended, its position did permit the desired walk. In the

Fig. 17

final sentence of his essay, Euler gave instructions for constructing such a walk in one's head rather than on paper: "Let those pairs of bridges which lead from one area to another be mentally removed, thereby considerably reducing the number of bridges; it is then an easy task to construct the required route across the remaining bridges, and the bridges which have been removed will not significantly alter the route found, as will become clear after a little thought."[23]

Alas, the possibility of taking a walk across Königsberg's bridges did not survive the Second World War. On the last few nights of August 1944, British air raids sent the city's new layout up in smoke. Only three of the eight bridges survived, and the city lost its name. In July 1946 it was renamed after the Soviet official and party functionary Mikhail Kalinin: Kaliningrad.

Today, Kaliningrad's traffic is a chaotic tangle – not because the city became a Russian island amid the Baltic states after the fall of the Soviet Union, but because its bridges are no longer at their poetically ordained locations in the weave of the city (Fig. 17).

4 Economies of thought

4.1 Diagnostic signs

In times of epidemic disease, diagnosis takes on a special role. The acts of classifying phenomena, determining a syndrome, and attributing symptoms – steps that are often jotted down by doctors on a sheet of paper – are supposed to constitute an individual clinical picture and establish the patient's condition. Such was the case at the start of the 1830s, when a cholera epidemic spread across all of Europe. Mass treatment demanded expedited prescription practices, and the homeopathic methods promoted by Samuel Hahnemann gained in prominence.[1]

In this then-new alternative medical model based on pathographic diagnostics, the sick person's symptoms are focused into a medicine, which is then given to the patient at an individually determined potency.[2] According to Hahnemann, the administration of low doses of a homeopathic remedy whose effects are perfectly matched to the symptoms of a *natural* illness (the "law of similars") creates an *artificial* illness that contains within itself "signatures" of the disease. These are then encountered by the "vital force," which responds by intensifying its natural defenses.[3] During the cholera outbreak, this homeopathic approach produced impressive results, making it instantly popular throughout Europe.

On September 11, 1832, on the eve of victory over the epidemic, the Russian homeopath Semën Korsakov, who had used the method successfully in Russia, wrote a letter to the Imperial

Academy of Sciences in Saint Petersburg, enclosing several diagrams of "intellectual machines." Korsakov viewed these machines, which were based on the tabular organization of homeopathic medicines, as "significant advances" in "human knowledge." By transforming *fixed ideas* into symbols and combining them, such machines could produce intellectual results: "If ... we were to express our 'ideas' with signs made up of actual physical bodies, possessing length and width and height, such signs would not merely be perceptible to several of our senses; as a consequence it would also be possible to discern similarities in the physical characteristics of the individual signs, which could be used to help solve purely intellectual problems."[4]

As Korsakov saw it, comparative operations on data sets could only be mechanized if the *plane of thought* were itself mechanized. This essay will consider the interrelationship between homeopathic and media-technological signs, as well as the mechanical execution of ideas, as illuminated by the designs for three of Korsakov's "homeoscopes."[5] At the time these devices were conceived, their practical implementation was nearly unimaginable, yet the logical processes they employed for classification, selection, and comparison would later be implemented by statistical and tabulating machines, and eventually by electronic computers.

4.2 The language of the "monster"

"My dear sir," Korsakov wrote to the secretary of the academy, Paul Fuss, "given that I have had the good fortune to have invented a new method of inquiry, the applications of which are of great importance, and being cognizant of the degree to which its publication may be beneficial to the attainments of human knowledge, I regard it as my duty to present to the academy the models of five such 'intellectual machines' of my invention, all of which function on the same principle." In the hope that these findings would be favorably received by the academy, Korsakov offered to "voluntarily forgo the greater part of the extraordinary privileges" he might legitimately have enjoyed "through the application of this heretofore unknown principle." Before concluding "with the greatest respect," the inventor and "most obedient and humble servant" suggested to the secretary that a committee be convened "for the evaluation of this principle, which forms a basis for the production of results beneficial to various activities of the mind."[6]

Following the early death of his father, a military engineer, Korsakov received a comprehensive education from his mother. During the campaign to repel Napoleon's invasion of Russia, Korsakov sustained an injury to his leg, which was plagued by painful inflammation for years thereafter. After learning of Hahnemann's new homeopathic methods from his cousin Ivan L'vov, a rheumatism specialist and landowner in the province of Saratov, Korsakov turned to homeopathy, healed himself, and subsequently came to see it as his duty, as it were, to disseminate the theoretical and practical knowledge of this alternative form of medical treatment. When the cholera epidemic broke out in 1829, he gave up his civil-service post as a statistician at the interior ministry in Saint Petersburg and moved to his estate not far outside the city, where he conducted studies of the disease, amassing as many as 11,725 cases between May 1829 and November 1834.

In the interest of constructing as accurate a clinical picture as possible, Hahnemann's *Organon*[7] – the foundational text of homeopathy – presents disease as a bodily phenomenon that is always expressed as a holistic complex of symptoms in the patient's subjective state, and thus in his or her verbal self-description. In adopting this perspective, Hahnemann, who began his intellectual career as a translator,[8] placed the focus on two fundamental methods of analysis: first, the patient's medical history, or "anamnesis," is compiled from what traditional medicine would regard as the colloquial aspects of the description of the case, and second, the written material from which the physician must derive the proving and healing symptoms is drawn from precisely these colloquial aspects. Language, in this constellation, is understood not as a representation of an illness (the characteristic view of traditional medicine, which regards the body as an emitter of signals), but rather as a set of *rules of usage*, the function and meaning of which loop themselves like a chain around what Hahnemann called the "thousand-headed monster of disease."[9]

By taking this approach to language, the homeopath could keep patients from adopting medical terminology, acting instead as their guide as they outlined their complaints in colloquial terms to be recorded by the attending physician. This alphabetic discretization of the stream of language became, for Korsakov, the basis for a possible mechanization of thought.[10] Yet it is precisely at this juncture, where meaning is understood as never located outside the level of language – that is, as always produced on the level of language[11] – that Hahnemann sees his calling as a translating healer. The doctor's systematizing, reasoning mind must confront the "thousand-headed monster" that conceals within itself neurasthenia, hysteria, hypochondria, mania, melancholy, idiocy, madness, falling sickness, convulsions, rickets, caries, and cancer, extracting from the sick person's word games a quasi-objective validity and thus an *idea* of a cure.

4.3 Tabular thinking

The reports Korsakov wrote on his cholera patients held particular value for the self-taught physician and statistician. In addition to conducting consultations, he also compiled his patient files, which he referred to as *tables*, into a comparative index in consideration of the fact that, in his view, "all our certain knowledge arises from the observation and comparison of facts." And since, as he wrote, humanity's ideas and inspirations are "recorded, conveyed, given permanence by words and writing, which are nothing more than mechanical operations of the mind,"[12] the tables he created for his patients, as one of the most important components of his idea machine, were placed in an *index table.*

Because Korsakov's invention was based on this homeoscopic table (Fig. 18), the descriptions of his machines begin with a detailed explanation of its workings:

> *g.g.g.g.* is a sturdy sheet of paper with strips *h.h.h.* etc. running lengthwise beneath it. The vertical columns *A-A, B-B, C-C,* etc. are marked on the surface of this sheet, crossed by the numbered horizontal rows *1-1, 2-2, 3-3,* etc. Each vertical column encompasses a complex idea, which is thus represented on the table. The details of these ideas are represented by rectangular holes in the paper created with a punch, shown here in black. All comparable details are found in the same horizontal row and can, as a consequence, be designated by that row's number. The names or labels of ideas *A, B, C, D,* etc. are inscribed on the lower or upper edge of the frame, or on the surface on which the table is placed. The edge sections *k k* and *k k* are raised half an inch above the surface of the table so that the homeoscope is contained between them while traversing it. Should one wish to use multiple tables treating different subjects, the descriptions of the complex ideas *A, B, C,* etc. are inscribed on the table itself rather than the edge sections *k k.*[13]

Korsakov was aware that his proposal placed him in a tradition, originating in the early modern era, of attempts to mechanize thought.[14] However, he was also aware that "despite the incalculable advantages of recording 'ideas' in material form by means of

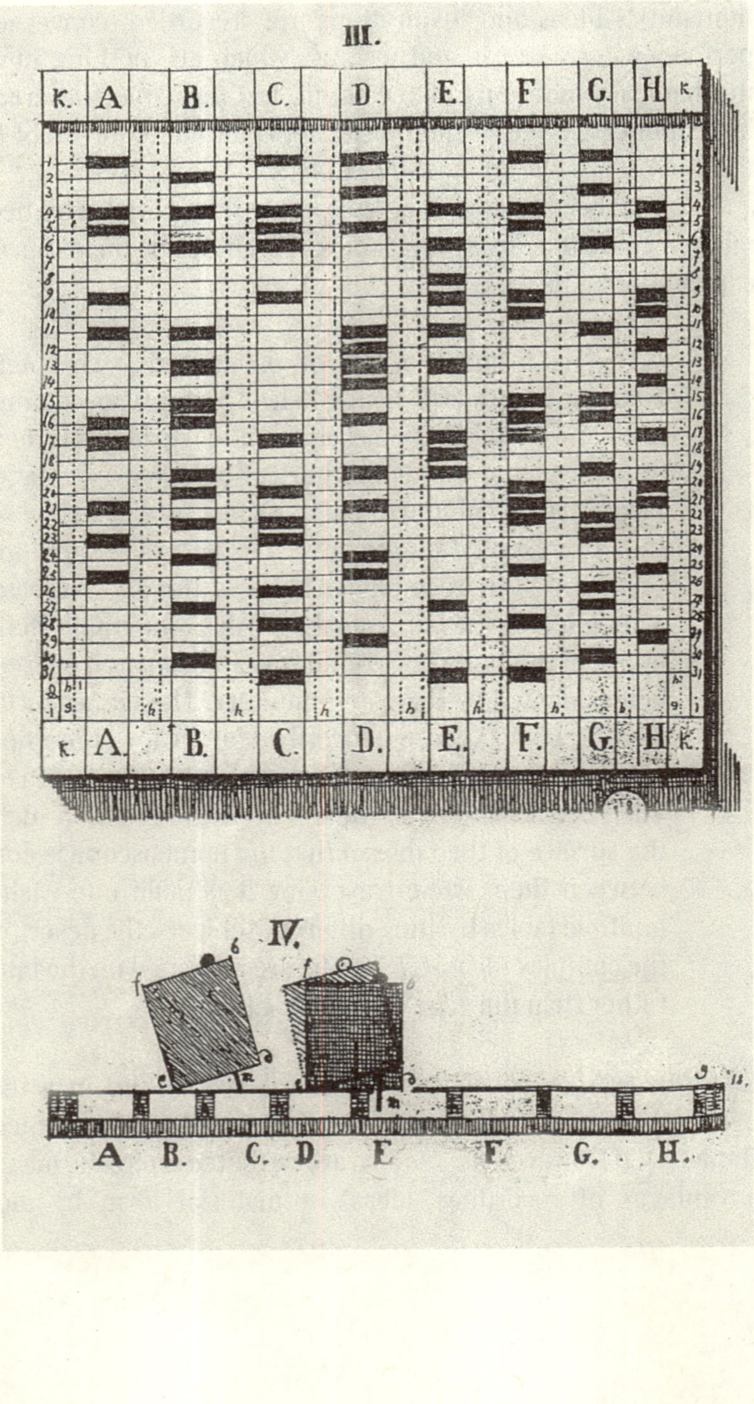

Fig. 18

writing, or with numbers, or especially through the use of clearly laid-out colored tables," no method then known was "capable of revealing, at a glance and in every detail, the results of a complicated comparison."[15] Korsakov sought to provide such an overview by combining the principle of the easy-to-understand table with mechanical procedures: "To do so, it is necessary merely to employ more corporeal symbols than those of which we ordinarily avail ourselves. Like all graphical methods, writing communicates with the mind solely by way of the eyes, eluding the potency of mechanical means."[16] To heighten that potency, and to turn a system of notation into a real symbolic machine, a hardware implementation, Korsakov proposed a three-dimensional apparatus. In his constructions, ideas are represented by symbols that truly are "real material bodies" possessing extension in length, breadth, and depth. Not only did these symbols create a previously nonexistent clarity *in thought*, in Korsakov's view, they also made it possible to discover similarities among symbols on the basis of their "physical characteristics."[17] Such symbols would thus be not only read but also placed, as physical objects, at the service of *thought*.

Accordingly, the homeoscope that accompanied the homeopathic table was a rectangular piece of wood (Fig. 19) whose length was equal to the height of the table. "This piece of wood is penetrated by as many pins as there are separate details on the table. Each pin corresponds to one of the table's numbered columns, and each pin's number is inscribed beside it on the homeoscope itself."[18] By correlating columns on the table with their corresponding numbers on the homeoscope, the rounded heads of the pins could convey the details of complex ideas to be compared against the ideas entered on the table.

To illustrate "the way in which this comparison takes place and how the result is to be expressed," Korsakov drew on an example from his day-to-day practice. He posited that "the complex ideas *A B C D* etc. represented on the table stand for the effects of various

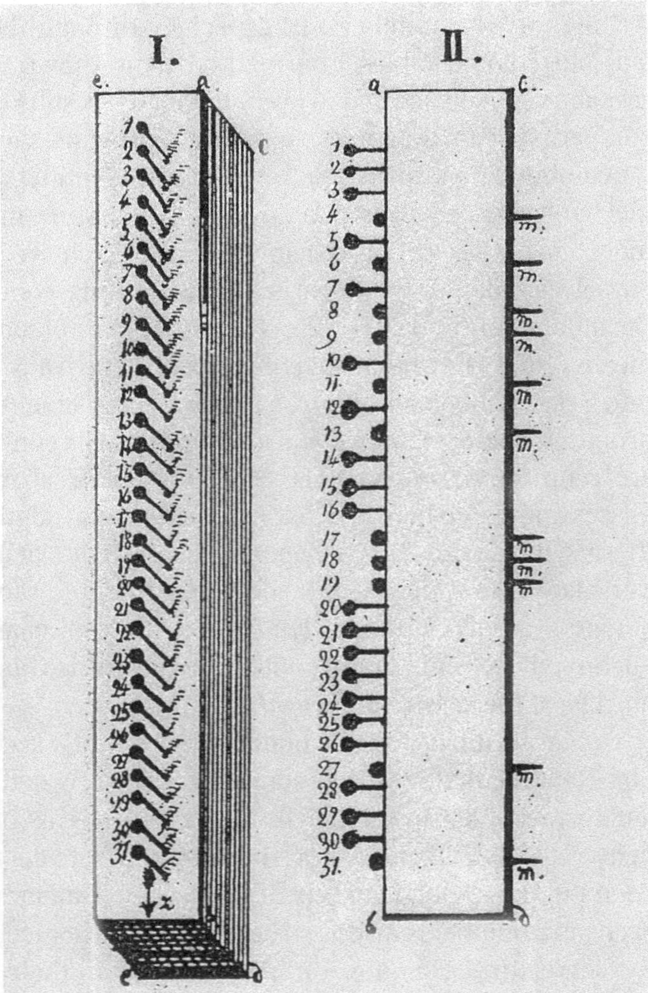

Fig. 19

medicines," with the numbered horizontal rows standing for various symptoms "for which these medicines are regarded as beneficial."[19]

The holes found in the column for medicine *A* would thus indicate that this medicine has a salutary effect for symptoms

> 1, 4, 5, 9, 16, 17, 21, 23, and 25, while those of medicine *B*, 2, 4, 6, 11, 13, 15, 16, 19, 20, 22, 24, 27, 30, indicate the same for that medicine, and so on for all the other columns, *C, D, E, F, G*, and *H*. Let us now assume that the complex ideas of an existing case consist of such symptoms as may be expressed by the numbers 4, 6, 8, 9, 11, 13, 17, 18, 19, 27, and 31. We prepare the homeoscope so that the points of pins *m* that correspond to these numbers protrude from it, and in this way a complete accounting of the illness is represented, on the instrument, by the protruding pins *m*, *m*, etc. We then lay the homeoscope between the two edge sections *k k* and *k k* with the points *m m* pressing downward upon the table, and we begin to slide the instrument from left to right, parallel to rows *AA*, *BB*, *CC*, etc. This movement continues, in our current example, as far as column *EE*: when the homeoscope arrives at that medicine, which corresponds to all the symptoms of our illness, it occurs that there is a hole below each protruding pin *m*, and consequently the piece of wood comprising the homeoscope, which is no longer supported by anything, now falls, each point entering a hole, and the instrument automatically comes to a stop. The result will be the same whether there are thirty-one or several hundred different symptoms represented on the table, and without taxing the mind or the memory in any way, we will have found what we were looking for – that is, the appropriate medicine for the case in question.[20]

Applied to the processes of thought, the purpose of the device Korsakov called the *linear homeoscope with immovable parts* was to peruse a great number of ideas represented on a table and quickly locate "those that correspond in every detail to a given idea," announcing the result by bringing the procedure to a halt. The use of this machine, whose search operation could be expanded to include multiple hundreds of details, would be "of exceptionally great benefit" for medicine, Korsakov wrote, “for once all the symptoms of an illness have been listed in detail, it can indicate with perfect accuracy the proper medicine for the case in question, and it can do this for any medical methodology desired.”[21] Viewed through the holes in the table, the patient becomes a data network, a transformation accompanied by the expectation that his or her illness can be healed by means of the compilation of statistics. On the table, the boundary between patient and illness shifts deep inside the body to be healed – which, in Korsakov’s proposals, is in keeping with human thought: “By employing such symbols to express each isolated detail of a particular idea, and by then mechanically bringing them into contact with other symbols of a similar nature, which, in similar fashion, expressed the details of a great number of other complex ideas, I arrived, through the resistance and the individual weight of these corporeal symbols, at the intellectual results I sought.”[22]

4.4 Contagious ideas

It was clear to Korsakov that language, in its *dynamic ambiguity*, leads inevitably to divergence. He therefore proposed that problems be broken down into discrete mechanizable steps so that all the details of a complex idea could be expressed in isolation. These material symbols could then be mechanically brought into logical, calculatory contact with other analog symbols that similarly represented the details of other complex ideas. The eminently physical weight and friction of these material symbols would bring the operator to the desired conceptual results. To achieve this effect, however, one first had to prepare an *array* – that is, the terms first had to be encoded. In the context of social symbolism, therefore, Korsakov’s patient files, with their descriptions of remedies and analyses of symptoms, upheld culturally specific *apparatuses of production*, “in which one is often required to mentally catalog a great number of varied ideas, which one must then recall and compare with other complicated ideas in order to form an opinion."[23] Korsakov knew, too, that in addition to the symbolic aspect of language there must also be a certain quantity of linking ideas, which needed to be conceived and generated with the help of some machine to keep us from drowning in the flood of data. It is precisely this operation, which produces certainty from the uncertain, thereby *extruding* a quantifiable transfer between past and future, that is embodied in Korsakov's designs:

> 1. Our mind, on its own, is unable to comprehend more than a few details at a single moment; by making use of this process, it is possible to comprehend thousands of details at once.
>
> 2. For the same reason, we cannot compare more than two objects at the same time, and if we turn our attention to a much larger number, we are compelled to execute the comparisons in no other way but sequentially; with the help of this process, we can compare a nearly limitless number of details at one and the same time, and we can absorb the results of this comparison in an instant.
>
> 3. Our memory, however happy it may be, is nonetheless not infallible, and this imperfection in its organization often causes us, without our knowing it, to lose sight of more or less important details. The material memory of my machines cannot fail, for it is the inevitable consequence of the physical qualities of matter, whose effect never abates.[24]

Korsakov's second homeoscope design (Fig. 20) provided the same functionality as the first; in addition, it could "instantly enumerate

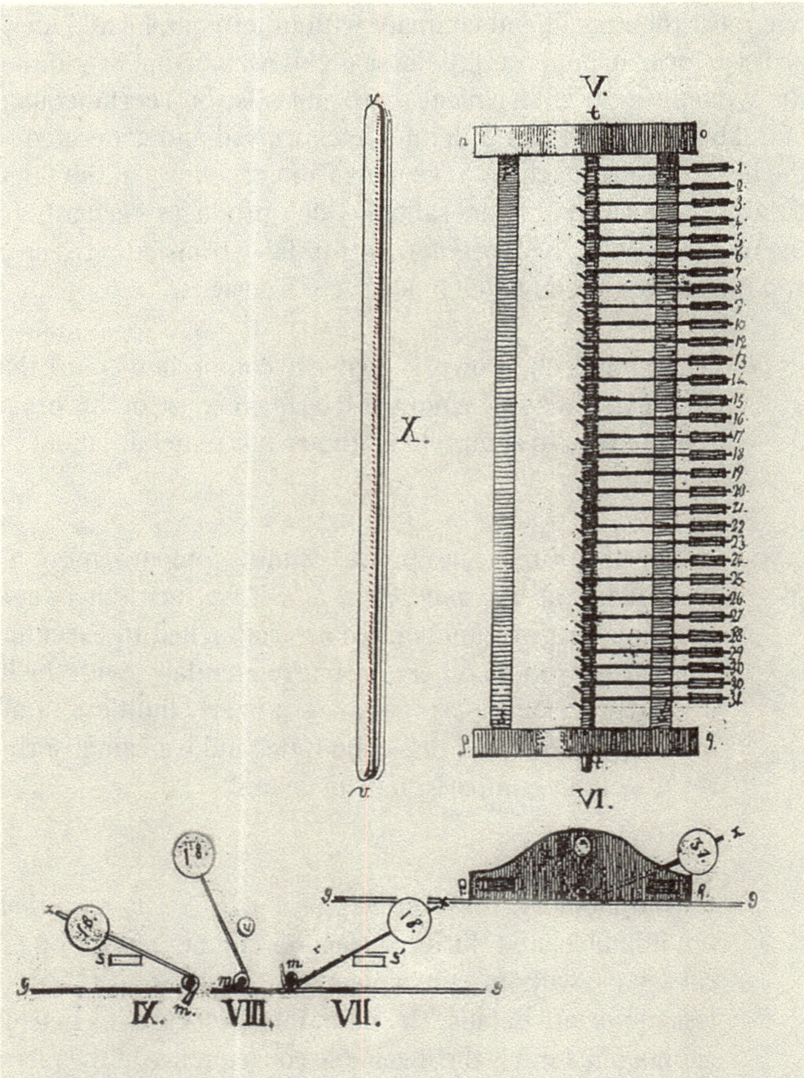

Fig. 20

and extract from a given idea all the details that are equivalent or not equivalent to the corresponding details of the other ideas on the table with which it is currently in contact."[25] Furthermore, the *linear homeoscope with movable parts*, as it was called, was equipped (as the name itself reveals) with moving styli that allowed all the numbered parts to rise and fall "depending on whether they are moving over the surface or a hole."[26] The idea of developing an algorithm to choose an appropriate course of action for every possible combination of concepts, symptoms, and indications presents the nature of thought as a process of both combinatorial analysis and probability calculation. The insights extruded in this process thus serve also to train the modes of perceptual experience necessary for the exploitation of remote fields of knowledge, unfolding the acquisition of knowledge in synchrony with an *economy of thought*. The thought process contained in this equivalence, a process of linking ideas – as opposed to the the mechanical form of all the parts and the connections between them – produces from the holes a knowledge-generating, self-evaluating machine that simultaneously conforms and gives rise to a transcendental conceptual schema.

This premise is quite clear in the third design, which is for a homeoscope that would instantly return "all the correspondences between two compared ideas, the details of which may be increased to ten thousand and far beyond" – even, through the use of graduated pins, "to more than a million."[27] Like the first two idea machines, this one is based on tables divided into squares by a number of straight lines (Fig. 21). The columns demarcated by the vertical lines are numbered, while the rows between the horizontal lines are labeled with letters. To illustrate the function of this machine, Korsakov turned once again to a medical example:

> Let us now assume that the letters *a b c d e f* etc. on the two tables represent the different parts of the body, or the *topography* of the human body, such as the head, nose, eyes,

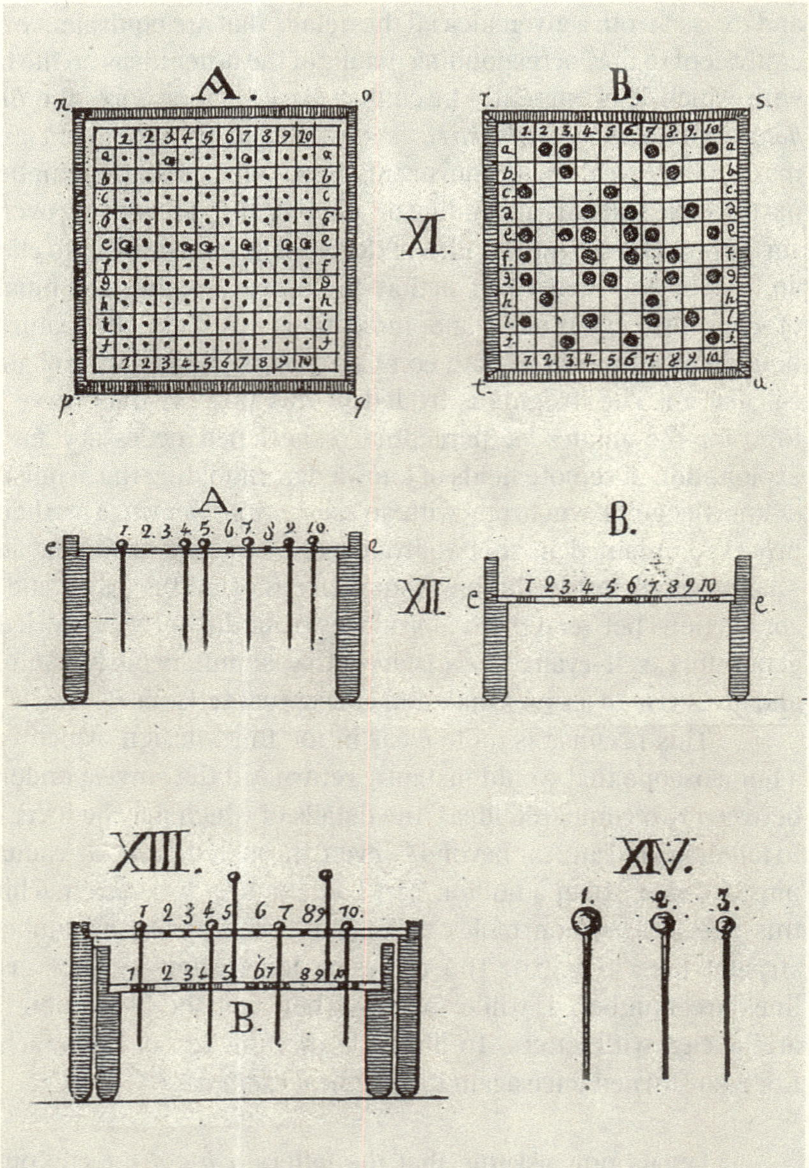

Fig. 21

stomach, etc., and that the numbers *1 2 3 4 5* etc. stand for the various types of morbid complaints to which our disposition is susceptible, which one might call *pathography*, e.g. swelling, redness, stabbing pain, cramping/tightness, heat, cold, weakness, etc. For example: if the letter *e* corresponds to the chest and the number *4* to tightness, then the square *e 4* stands for *tightness in the chest*; and by placing a pin through the hole in the middle of this square on the top table, one may indicate the presence of this symptom and others. In this way, ten thousand different variants of a disease can be represented on a table one hundred squares high and wide. All the details of a given case, however numerous they may be, can thus be marked with pins on the top table.[28]

In seeking to represent the different variants of a disease, Korsakov's concern is not to shine a light into the patient, illuminating his or her unconscious; rather, inside the self-describing patient it becomes clear to him that his gaze calls forth the fundamental phenomenological qualities of perception, and of knowledge in general. As a consequence of the ambiguity of the linguistic sign, the chain of meaning can never be completed; some recognition of this fact must lie behind Korsakov's statement, quoted above, that, "despite the incalculable advantages of recording 'ideas' in material form by means of writing, with numbers, and especially through the use of colorful, clearly laid-out tables, none of the methods now known are capable of revealing, at a glance and in every detail, the results of a complicated comparison."[29]

4.5 New forms of thought

In its interweaving of religious, political, and technological perceptual regimes, the time of the 1831–32 cholera epidemic not only represents a profitable (and, as the era demonstrated, regeneratively linked) poetological business in dead souls,[30] it also marks the cultural origins of a mystery that would give rise to a religion of science while remaining unsolved until the advent of bacteriology sixty years later.[31] The unrest that arose in connection with the outbreak was not merely a matter of social protests and political conflicts; it was also a massive reaction to the restrictive medical-regulatory body politics by which, since the dawn of the nineteenth century, the role of the sick person had come to be circumscribed.[32] The invention of new ways of thinking, as realized in Korsakov's machines, was thus connected to a development that might be described as the renovation of humanity in the process of industrialization. The disorganized statements of the patient become the grid of a card; from the collation of these cards spring poetologies of knowledge that might, by leading someone to design an idea machine, insert themselves onto the plateau of reality. Hence Korsakov's assertion that his method could be applied "not only to the sciences in general, but also to the business of everyday life."[33]

The indifference of the history of science and technology to Korsakov's concepts was already apparent in the scorn expressed by the scholars of the day:

> Were the author to go to the trouble of completing his homeopathic table, incorporating every pathological symptom for every part of the human body and every remedy, he would surely discover that such a table – in all likelihood the smallest any branch of the sciences might require – would be so extensive that it would have to be printed in pocket size; to use it at the bedside of a patient would be absolutely impossible. And furthermore, we are ignoring the fact that a mechanical method of treatment would completely destroy the patient's trust – and the physician's capacity for thought. [34]

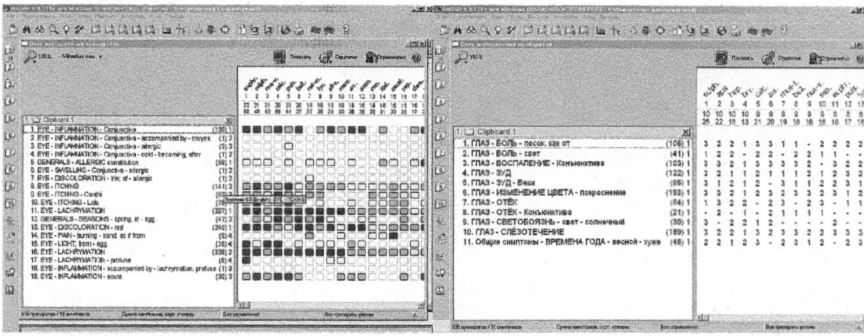

Fig. 22

The ideas extruded from the holes mark out a pathway in a historical constellation in which the mathematization of medicine is accompanied by the increasing dominance of diagrammatic cultural technologies. In constructing knowledge by means of mechanical operations, Korsakov's idea machine became, for its operator, an "interlocutor" that inserted itself, like a punch card, between one's actions and the conscious observation of those actions, and which possessed the advantage of being *transcodable* to various branches of knowledge, of extruding the unknown from the known. The Korsakovian mathematical tool kit – the analytical method of probability calculation embodied by the homeoscopes – generated a pattern whose conceptual analogue is used in the computer programs of today's homeopathy to select the right course of treatment (Fig. 22). And if it can be said that the unconscious is at work in the design of technology, then it is precisely this unconscious, unnoticed by its contemporaries in the hour of its emergence, that has embedded itself in the holes of the archives.

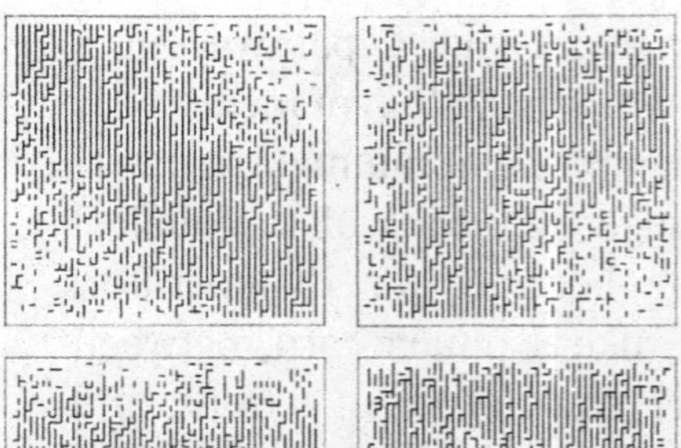

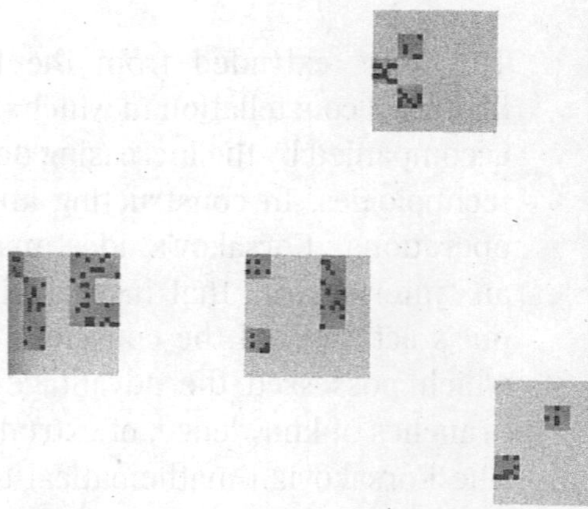

Fig. 23

5 Chains of chance: a convoluted history of pattern recognition

5.1 In the face of the irregular

When black grids appear out of the void and lines suddenly change direction, chance is at work on a composition. Consider two pictures that could not be more different and yet are also very similar – both contain four squares, but with different patterning: in the first one, a riot of angles fill the squares' surfaces (fig. 23, left), while in the second the surfaces are graced by rectangular pixels in varying shades of gray (fig. 23, right). The first is an artwork by Frieder Nake, the second a "plate" by Benoît Mandelbrot illustrating a scientific model. But what constitutes the essential identity of these pictures?

Mandelbrot's book *The Fractal Geometry of Nature* famously begins with a "manifesto": "There is a fractal face to the geometry of nature." In this "scientific essay," he reveals that many forms in nature obey one simple principle: self-similarity, or, to use Mandelbrot's term, *scale invariance*. Working from this principle – according to which an object's pattern reappears again and again when that object is infinitely enlarged (scaled) – fractal geometry unveils nature's "hidden face."[1]

The following is an attempt to retrace "the path to fractals," which itself resembles the curves analyzed in Mandelbrot's book. He offers an enigmatic sketch of that path in the book's epilogue, in which he speaks of a land (which he does not name) to which he has had a lifelong connection, of a book he discovered in the wastebasket of a "pure" mathematician, of regularities in word frequencies and the birth of mathematical linguistics, of accidents, probabilities, and chains – and of the fact that, although these phenomena belong to the past, he has not stopped feeling their aftereffects. The common thread in all of it consists of various techniques of inference and the order-generating chance processes associated with them. It was out of these that the "geometric face" of the theory of scale invariance emerged, that it "grew in importance and gave size to fractal geometry."[2]

5.2 Chance as tool

To establish the concept of a chain of random variables, the Russian mathematician A. A. Markov appeared before the Physical-Mathematical Division of the Imperial Academy of Sciences in Saint Petersburg on January 23, 1913 to present the results of an experiment on the letters of the Russian alphabet. With his findings, which were published soon thereafter in the bulletin of the academy,[3] the probability theorist hoped to cause as much of a stir in the early twentieth century as Mandelbrot's "scientific essay" would in its latter half.[4]

And in fact, the radicality of Markov's experimental approach cannot be overstated. Well aware that it was the two hundredth anniversary of the publication of Jakob Bernoulli's classic treatise on probability theory,[5] Markov set about deconstructing Russian poetry. The object of his statistical investigation was *Eugene Onegin*, the Romantic novel in verse by the Russian literary giant Alexander Pushkin (fig. 24). Ignoring punctuation marks and spaces, Markov arranged the book's first twenty thousand letters into two hundred blocks of sharply printed characters, each block laid out in ten columns and ten rows.

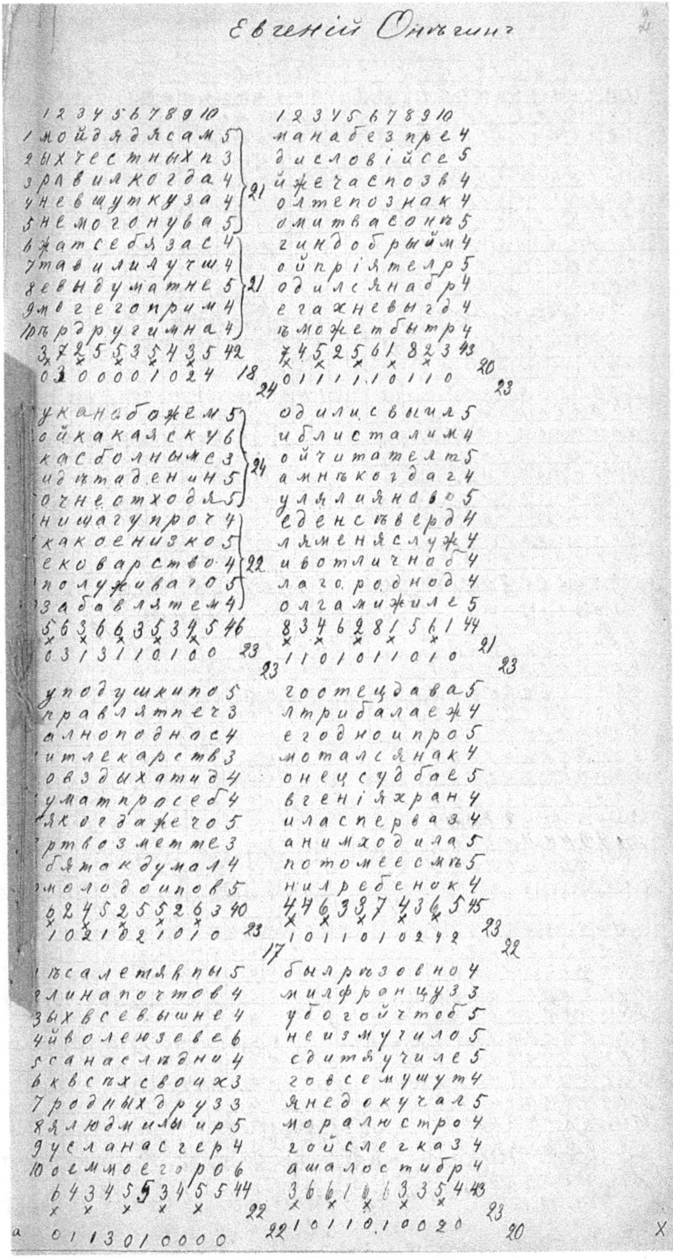

Евгеній Онѣгинъ

1 2 3 4 5 6 7 8 9 10 — 1 2 3 4 5 6 7 8 9 10
1 мойдядясам 5 — манабезпре 4
2 ыхчестныхп 3 — дисловійсе 5
3 правилкогда 4 — йжечаспозв 4
4 невшуткуза 4 — олтепознак 4
5 немогонува 5 — дмитвасонъ 5
6 жатсебязас 4 — гиндобрыйм 4
7 тавилилучш 4 — ойпріятелр 5
8 евндуматне 5 — одилсянабр 4
9 мвгегоприм 4 — егажневыгд 4
10 ърдругимна 4 — ъможетбытр 4
(21, 21)
3 7 2 5 5 3 5 4 3 5 42 — 7 4 5 2 5 6 1 8 2 3 43
0 3 0 0 0 0 1 0 2 4 18 24 — 0 1 1 1 1 1 0 1 1 0 20 23

уканабожем 5 — одилисвыил 5
ойкакаяскуб — иблисталим 4
касбольныме 3 — ойчитателт 5
идътаденин 5 — амнъкогдаг 4
очнеотходя 5 — улялиянаво 5
нищагупроч 4 — еденсъверд 4
какоенизко 5 — ляменяслуж 4
ековарство 4 — ивотличнаб 4
полуживаго 5 — лагородно д 4
забавлятем 4 — олгамижиле 5
(24, 22)
5 6 3 6 6 3 5 3 4 5 46 — 8 3 4 6 2 8 1 5 6 1 44
0 3 1 3 1 1 0 1 0 0 23 23 — 1 1 0 1 0 1 1 0 1 0 21 23

уподушкипо 5 — гоотецдава 5
правлятнеч 3 — лтрибалаеж 4
алноподнас 4 — егоднаипро 5
итлекарств 3 — моталсянак 4
овздыхатид 4 — онецсудбае 5
уматпросеб 4 — вгеніяхран 4
якогдажечо 5 — иласперваз 4
ртвозметте 3 — анимходила 5
бятакдумал 4 — потомеесмъ 5
молодоипов 5 — нилребенок 4
6 2 4 5 2 5 5 2 6 3 40 — 4 4 6 3 3 7 4 3 6 5 45
1 0 2 1 0 2 1 0 1 0 23 17 — 1 0 1 1 0 1 0 2 4 2 23 22

1 ъсалетявпы 5 — былрьзовно 4
2 линапочтов 4 — милфранцуз 3
3 ыхвсевышне 4 — убогойчтоб 5
4 йволеюзеве 6 — неизмучило 5
5 санаслъдни 4 — сдитяучиле 5
6 квспхсвоих 3 — говсемушут 4
7 родныхдруз 3 — янедокучал 5
8 ялюдмилыир 5 — моралнстро 4
9 усланасгер 4 — гойслегказ 4
10 оеммоегоро 6 — ашалостибр 4
6 4 3 4 5 5 3 4 5 5 44 — 3 6 6 1 6 6 3 3 5 4 43
0 1 1 3 0 1 0 0 0 0 22 22 — 1 0 1 1 0 1 0 0 2 0 23 20

Fig. 24

These gridlike arrays became a visual and theoretical laboratory on paper in which Markov discerned a system of *chained values*: a model, consisting of sequences of random variables, in which each found occurrence contains the precondition of the next. Just as each of the numerous links in a chain is connected only to the link before it, Markov notes, the probability of each occurrence is dependent only on the preceding occurrence, and not on the many others.

Markov's interpretive dissection of *Eugene Onegin* makes clear that his aim was to produce a model from which one might derive the probabilities underlying the alternation between vowels and consonants that is typical of Russian as well as English and many other languages (fig. 25). Given any letter, one would be able to make predictions about the letter to follow. In this way, Markov transformed language into a chained array that contained within it the basis of a newly focused probability theory.

5.3 The biometry of literary style

Markov's study did not have to wait long for a response. In 1915, Nikolai Alexandrovich Morozov published his own analysis of literary style. Morozov's "linguistic spectra," as they are called in the title of his essay, were intended as "a way to distinguish plagiarism from the genuine works of a known author," and their sophisticated linkings were meant to provide objective proof of Markov's model.[6] Morozov, a poet, writer, and linguist who would go on to become an honorary member of the Russian Academy of Sciences, had acquired his scientific knowledge through amateur experimentation in cosmology, physics, chemistry, biology, geophysics, and meteorology, from which he concluded that true scientific accuracy is based entirely on statistics.[7]

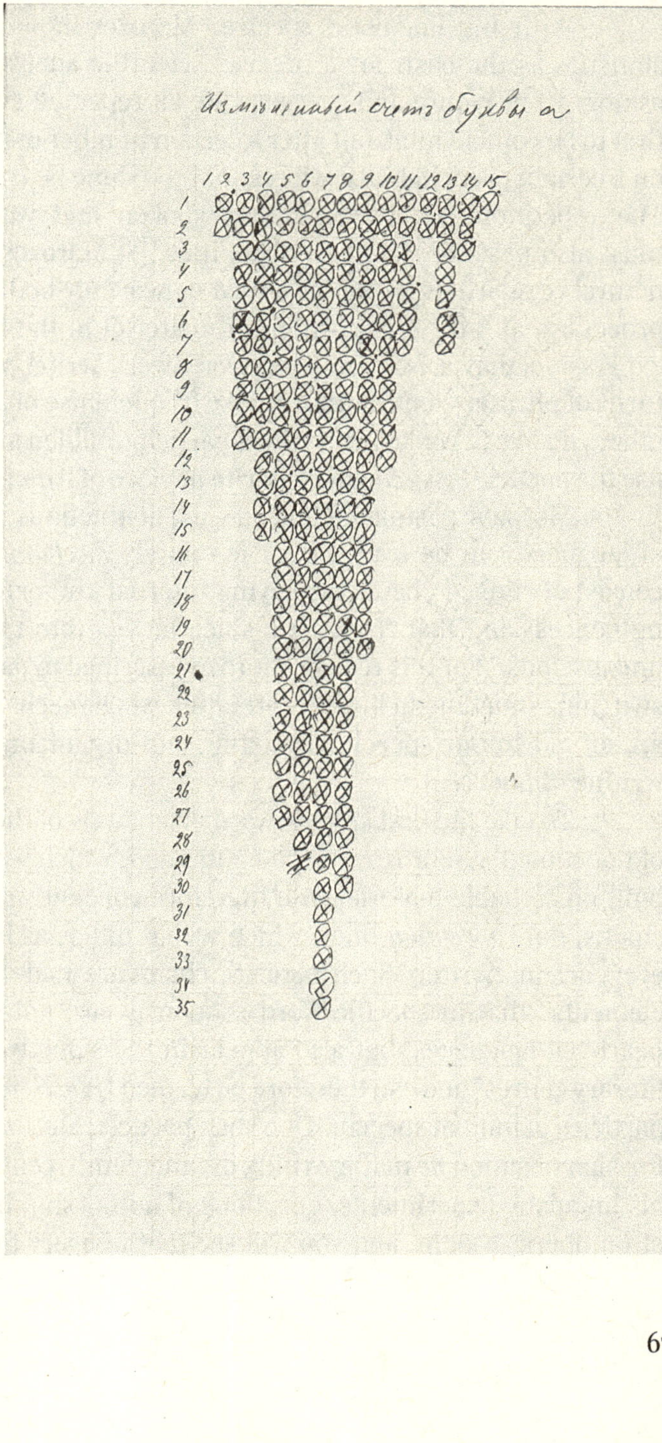

Fig. 25

With his linguistic spectra, Morozov now sought to use statistics as the basis for a precise, scientific analysis of language, asking: "If in nature and everyday life all repeated events appear at first to be coincidental, but after a certain number of repetitions take on a certain predictability, why cannot the same be true of language? The repetitions of words in our spoken and written language must also possess various probabilities."[8] Morozov saw the same natural regularities he had observed in heavenly bodies, mechanical processes, and the composition of matter[9] in the individuality of expression that arises from the way every writer uses particular turns of phrase: "Some authors make frequent use of the word *which*; others dislike it, replacing it with a participle added at the end. Some use the particle *between*; others write in place of it *amid* or *within*."[10]

Morozov postulated that all such distinctions in the structure of language can be traced back to "purely *mechanical causes*" that consist of "linked chains displaying internal and external linguistic influences" and that "have long since moved into the realm of the unconscious." For this reason, Morozov ascribed to particles a sort of switching function. In his interpretation, such mechanical processes are an aid to our speech, regulating and organizing it, and to the writing of poets.[11]

To take the first steps toward an analysis of the authorship of old documents, Morozov needed a method, which would have to be built on "reliable material." He therefore concentrated on *linguistic* chains, not *conceptual* ones, which would differ, as he noted, "with every original writer." Such linguistic chains are made up of individual elements "that in specific word sequences are not only typical of nearly all languages, but also appear in the same way in nearly all literary genres" and can therefore be termed "*functional* or *organizing* particles of human speech." One such particle, Morozov wrote, is the Russian negation *ne* in the writing of nineteenth-century authors. In his linguistic experiments, questions of authorship became a game of numbers: "Count, and you will see that in every thousand words in Tolstoy this [negation] appears on average somewhat fewer than twenty times, in Pushkin and Gogol roughly twenty times, and in Turgenev a bit more than in his predecessors, sometimes more than thirty times. In general, the word's fluctuations fall into the range of twelve to thirty-five times per thousand words, always depending on a particular writer's proclivity for negation."[12]

Morozov concluded that the use of "the negative particle *ne* depends in large part on individual variation" and thus dictates the structure of each author's language.[13] This appears to contradict the proposition that language patterns can be predicted from the logic of the chain: in Morozov's model, the author's uniqueness is mirrored in the uniqueness of his written work. Morozov's implicit criticism of Markov becomes all the more apparent when, at the end of his introduction, he states: "Unfortunately, you will not be able to arrive at any conclusion if all the words are written together without spaces or punctuation."[14]

Despite this objection, Morozov was directly indebted to Markov. He not only took up his predecessor's experiment, he was likewise driven by a desire to visualize chance. Indeed, the graphics he produced in his pattern experiments led him, in much the same way as Markov, to identify authors' textual quirks and locate them within linguistic spectra (fig. 26). But even though Morozov's research was based on images of chance, it was nonetheless published as "linguistic analysis."[15] To differentiate his spectra, Morozov broke them down into prepositional, subjunctive, pronominal, and other syntactic groupings, superimposing the corresponding graphs upon them. At this point, the image takes on an authority that seems to exceed the expertise of the linguist. Morozov's superimposition of the graphs makes this clear: "With a simple glance at the prepositional spectrum of any work by Pushkin that may have been erroneously attributed to Gogol, we would have recognized the inaccuracy of such an assertion and accordingly expressed the suspicion that the work was likely one of Pushkin's."[16]

Спектръ и" — не — и'.

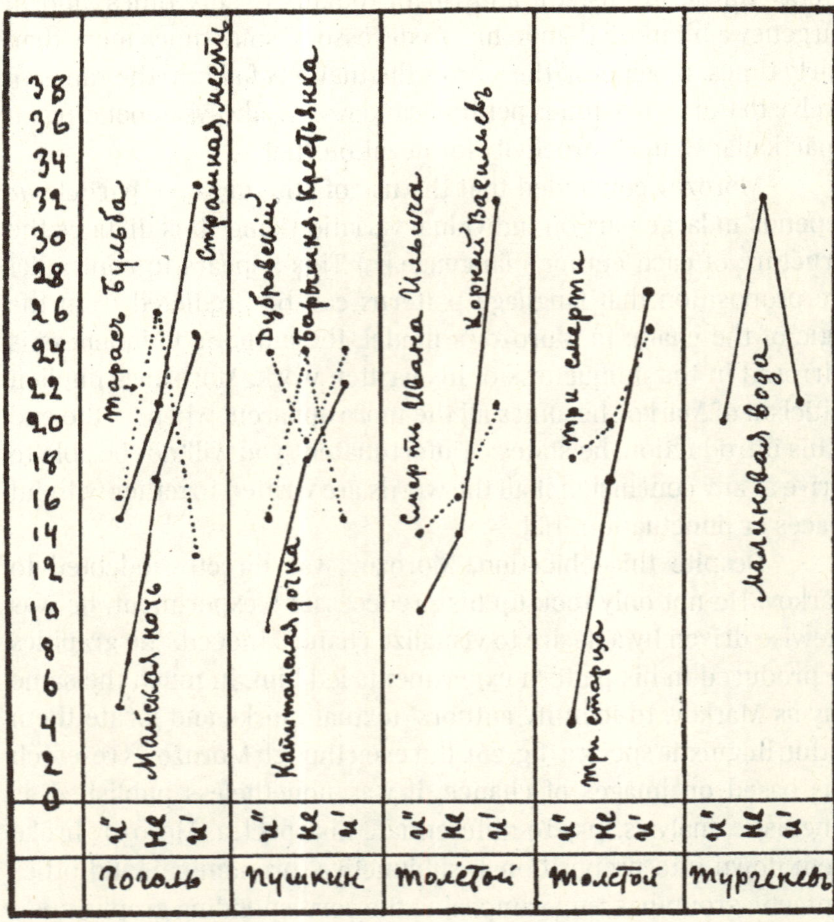

Fig. 26

However, as a statistician, Morozov knew that only averages can be compared in this manner; to advance an irrefutable proposition, he would need more than his overlays alone. For the moment, though, he limited himself to a thousand words, from which he calculated a *mean* for the particles. He identified this mean as a natural value that determined the author's "syllabic physiognomy."[17] Morozov's spectra were defined with sufficient clarity both to reveal the author's signature in his own works and to set him apart from other writers. Here, *physiognomy* is not a mere figure of speech: the visible countenance of language, represented by an overlay of graphs, became a mark of individuality with which genuine authors could be distinguished from impostors. Chance is not without order. When Mandelbrot later felt that he was looking into the "fractal face of nature," he was translating this same experience into images and a theory of his own.

True to the principle of the chain reaction, Markov, the man who originated the notion, responded to Morozov's provocation a year later. Morozov's idea was not fundamentally wrong, Markov averred, but its implementation should by no means be based on a subjective sense of literary style, nor was it enough to count a mere thousand words as Morozov had done. He then proceeded to dismantle, on solid literary-mathematical grounds, Morozov's proof of the spectra: his example of the negative particle. Markov, who never tired of counting, used Morozov's own method against him, demonstrating the instability of Morozov's linguistic spectra, in comparison to his own chain sampling, by tripling the number of negations counted for each author. The type of precise scientific analysis of language that Morozov had attempted, Markov declared, would have to be built on a foundation of mathematical statistics, which presupposed the counting of several thousand sentences, words, syllables, and letters.[18] Since the invention of the computer, automatic speech recognition has been achieved on just such a basis, its fundamental problem being the establishment of a connection between sequences of spoken sounds and the words that correspond to them.

5.4 The principle of least effort

The pattern systems of the 1910s, which were based on the frequencies of letters and individual words, were taken up again in the 1930s by George Kingsley Zipf. A lecturer at Harvard, Zipf extended Markov's and Morozov's methods in his own research, investigating the frequency of words in various languages and thereby identifying new linguistic patterns.[19] By arranging the words in a language according to their frequency of appearance, Zipf arrived at various mathematical constants: for example, he found that the more common a word is, the shorter it is, and that a word's frequency is also influenced by its age.[20]

These laws would eventually find their way into the major study on communication that Zipf published in 1949 under the title *Human Behavior and the Principle of Least Effort*. Here he applied his mathematical findings to people's linguistic practice (i.e. speech habits): frequently used words are shortened, while greater length tends to be tolerated in less common words. This observation was the source of the Zipfian model of communication: every speaker seeks to convey his or her message with the least possible effort. This, however, produces a discrepancy, for the listener or reader on the other end of the channel wants to decipher that message with the least possible effort as well.[21] It is only when these two opposing principles are brought into balance that communication is possible.

Among other things, it was a review of this book that led Mandelbrot to fractals: "This empirical regularity concerning word frequencies had come to my attention through a book review. The event seems too symbolic to be true, but the review in question had been retrieved from a 'pure' mathematician's wastebasket, for light reading on the Paris subway."[22] The pure mathematician was Mandelbrot's uncle, Szolem Mandelbrojt, with whom Mandelbrot frequently stayed between 1945 and 1947 while studying at the École polytechnique, and whom he visited regularly in Paris while working on his doctorate

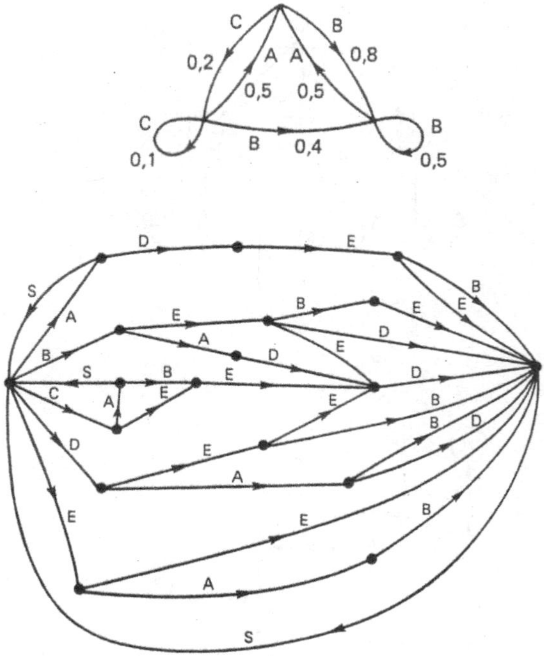

Fig. 27

thereafter. The reviewer, meanwhile, turns out to have been the mathematician Joseph Walsh, who in 1949 discussed the study of his Harvard colleague Zipf in *Scientific American*. As chance would have it, in his dissertation[23] Mandelbrot was combining known methods of linguistic analysis with Norbert Wiener's cybernetics and John von Neumann's game theory, which were also in vogue at that time. By analyzing language from a macrolinguistic perspective rather than a microlinguistic one in his study, Mandelbrot hoped to become "the Kepler of mathematical linguistics."[24]

While placing himself in the Markovian tradition, Mandelbrot pointed out that the Russian's theory of dependent random variables had since been expanded by a series of new concepts and interpretations that had changed the shape of his chains. This

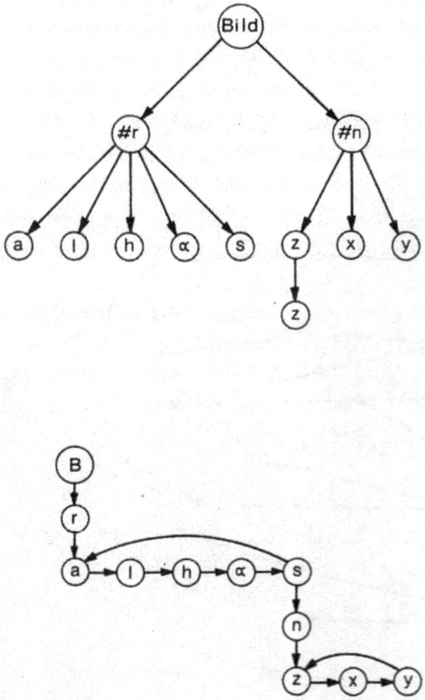

Fig. 28

evolution was due mainly to the work of Claude Shannon, who in 1947 showed that the Markov chain was still useful as a mathematical model for the theory of information transmission. As Shannon's illustration shows (fig. 27, top), information to be communicated with numbers can be quantified by means of a chain of code elements. Shannon turned to the theory of Markov chains because, as he wrote, "the main point at issue is the effect of statistical knowledge about the source in reducing the required capacity of the channel, by the use of proper encoding of the information"[25] (fig. 27, bottom).

When Mandelbrot then further expanded this model for his own purposes, the critical difference in his approach to ordering signs was the introduction of a space: a sign that cannot appear within a word. It was an element that mathematicians such as

Markov and Shannon had omitted from their language models, but that linguists such as Morozov and Zipf had reintroduced. Because a space marks the boundaries between words, it is not dependent on adjacent letters; as a result, the individual word becomes the central interval of chance.[26] In the terminology of probability theory, this means that language displays a high degree of self-similarity – and here Mandelbrot recognized the scale invariance that would become one of the fundamental principles of his later work.

This can also be seen in Mandelbrot's implementation of Hoyle's cosmological model on the basis of random "curdling" of forms in a grid (fig. 23, right): no matter where or in which shade of gray the grids appear, they are determined by transition probabilities. The same is true of the angles in Frieder Nake's *walk-through-raster* series (fig. 23, left, and fig. 28), in which a Markov chain of random events decides for the drawing program where a given transition will occur.[27] In Mandelbrot's Hoyle visualizations, random events – from coin tosses to birth rates to the calculated distribution of galaxies and their resulting densities – are determined by transition probabilities. Thus it is not only the codes that are linked together, but also the sources. It was for this reason that Mandelbrot wrote at the end of *The Fractal Geometry of Nature*: "At a critical point in my life ... I read a wise review of *Human Behavior* by the mathematician J. L. Walsh. By only mentioning what was good, this review influenced greatly my early scientific work, and its indirect influence continues. Therefore, I owe a great debt to Zipf through Walsh."[28] If not for those earlier attempts, beginning with Markov, to make visible the chains of chance, Mandelbrot would not have been able to recognize the "fractal face of nature."

6 The pounding of hammers

6.1 Poetic groundwork

> A man with knowledge, but without ability –
> is a machine without a motor.
>
> *Aleksei Gastev*

In 1924, the Futurist hymnodist Aleksei Kapitonovich Gastev proposed building a series of monuments:

> To the protozoan — who sparked the reaction,
> To the dog — our greatest friend, who calls us to practice,
> To the ape — that whirlwind of vigorous movement,
> To the hand — the magical intuition of will and work,
> To the savage — with his hammer of stone,
> To the tool — a banner of the will,
> To the machine — which teaches us speed and precision,
> And to all who dare to call for the transformation
> Of man.[1]

This memorial manifesto, posted on a signboard outside the Central Institute of Labor (CIT) – which Gastev had founded, and which introduced the teachings of biomechanics and the system of Taylorism into factories, theaters, and sports stadiums after the revolution[2] – clearly bears the stamp of its author. For in his visions of work, Gastev embodied a duality: as a poet, he helped to draft a futuristic vision of the new machine man, yet he was also an agent of that harsh, subrepresentative ergometric discourse of capitalism known as Taylorism.[3] The system he developed at his institute for the "scientific organization of work" (*nauchnaya organizatsiya truda*) extended into areas more commonly associated with the Russian avant-garde and the more radical manifestations of Constructivism, as well as the regulatory measures of the new government's New Economic Policy.[4] Thus, after the October Revolution, Gastev undertook a reorganization of all the disciplines he considered essential for the country's new rulers. The CIT became a laboratory of the quotidian, where human perception and the human body were investigated in relation to physiological and psychological criteria.[5] After the founding of the CIT, which Gastev considered his "last artistic production" (*posledneye khudozhestvennoye proizvedeniye*), he restricted himself, as a writer, to journalistic and scientific texts.[6] Gastev's visions for the rational reorganization of work were inspired by the economic "system" of labor developed by Frederick Winslow Taylor.[7] Isolated workflows, set sequences, the synchronization of the worker's movements with the pattern set by the machine, the optimization of the rhythms of work via shift systems – these were the principles of Taylorism, which sought to optimize labor, management, and business in accordance with a purely scientific approach, thereby creating prosperity for all. A system in which Lenin, after the October Revolution, placed great hopes:

> The task that the Soviet government must set the people in all its scope is – learn to work. The Taylor system, the last word of capitalism in this respect, like all capitalist progress, is a combination of the refined brutality of bourgeois exploitation and a number of the greatest scientific achievements in the field of analysing mechanical motions during work, the elimination of superfluous and awkward

> motions, the elaboration of correct methods of work, the introduction of the best system of accounting and control, etc. The Soviet Republic must at all costs adopt all that is valuable in the achievements of science and technology in this field. The possibility of building socialism depends exactly upon our success in combining the Soviet power and the Soviet organisation of administration with the up-to-date achievements of capitalism. We must organise in Russia the study and teaching of the Taylor system and systematically try it out and adapt it to our own ends.[8]

Gastev's ideas about reorganizing the factory space to allow for the constant training, monitoring, and quantification of the worker's movements – and, in particular, for the retraining of the worker – were influenced by Taylorist views. His regulated and, more importantly, *preplanned* work routines and movement sequences were intended not just to maximize output, but also to create the necessary *settings* for a fusion of man and machine. Mechanical economy and efficiency would, it was thought, shape a new and virtuous human consciousness with the goal of selfless devotion to work and to the collective, the melting of the individual into the working mass: "The worker is organically melded with the machinery of the entire factory."[9] In this context it becomes clear for the first time that Gastev's poetological theories were not limited simply to worker productivity; rather, they formed a foundation of inventive rules upon which the "new man" would draw himself erect. This essay will focus on the ways in which Gastev constructed the action of hammering – constructions in which the founder of the organization of work in the Soviet Union detected reverberations of the fundamental elements of experimental psychology and the physiology of movement, and from which, in his envisioning, the protocybernetic form of the entire Gastevian program would rise to become a system of culture.

6.2 Constructions of a hammer blow

The prerequisites — or, to use Gastev's terminology, the *presets*[10] – for every successful work operation consist of statics and dynamics (Fig. 29). Statics is understood as "a beneficial positioning of the 'framework' of the living machine" in order to achieve "a deactivation of the muscles and their contraction" to the extent necessary for "stability when shifting the center of gravity and resistance while hammering"; the dynamics of work, meanwhile – or, in the case of hammering, the "biomechanics of the hammer blow" – comprises an "increase in ability and the triumphant acquisition of routines, after mastering which the worker-trainee moves from one accomplishment to the next, ultimately achieving proficiency."[11]

To introduce the hammering action, Gastev created a series of "dispositions" that gave an "indication of the movements of work," an "outline executed in the simplest calisthenic movements."[12] These included exercises for grasping and swinging the tool (Fig. 30), in which "the index finger and the thumb laid upon it function as a pivot, while the middle, ring, and little finger take on the role of a motor."[13] Extended to the wrist, upper arm, and shoulder, these exercises were intended to impart "purposefulness and measure" to the trainee's movements, revealing the construction of those movements and, as a result, "providing an introductory education in all pounding movements of the worker."[14]

From these presets and calisthenic exercises, Gastev next moved to the construction of the hammering action. As a person who viewed machine assembly as the foundation of all possible formations, he broke down the pounding movement into its mechanical elements in order to introduce *bone-lever movements* – simple ones at first, then more challenging ones: "By forcing specific bone levers to work, we also force the corresponding flexor and extensor muscles to work." Training such bone-lever movements would result in a more efficient use of muscular and neural energy,

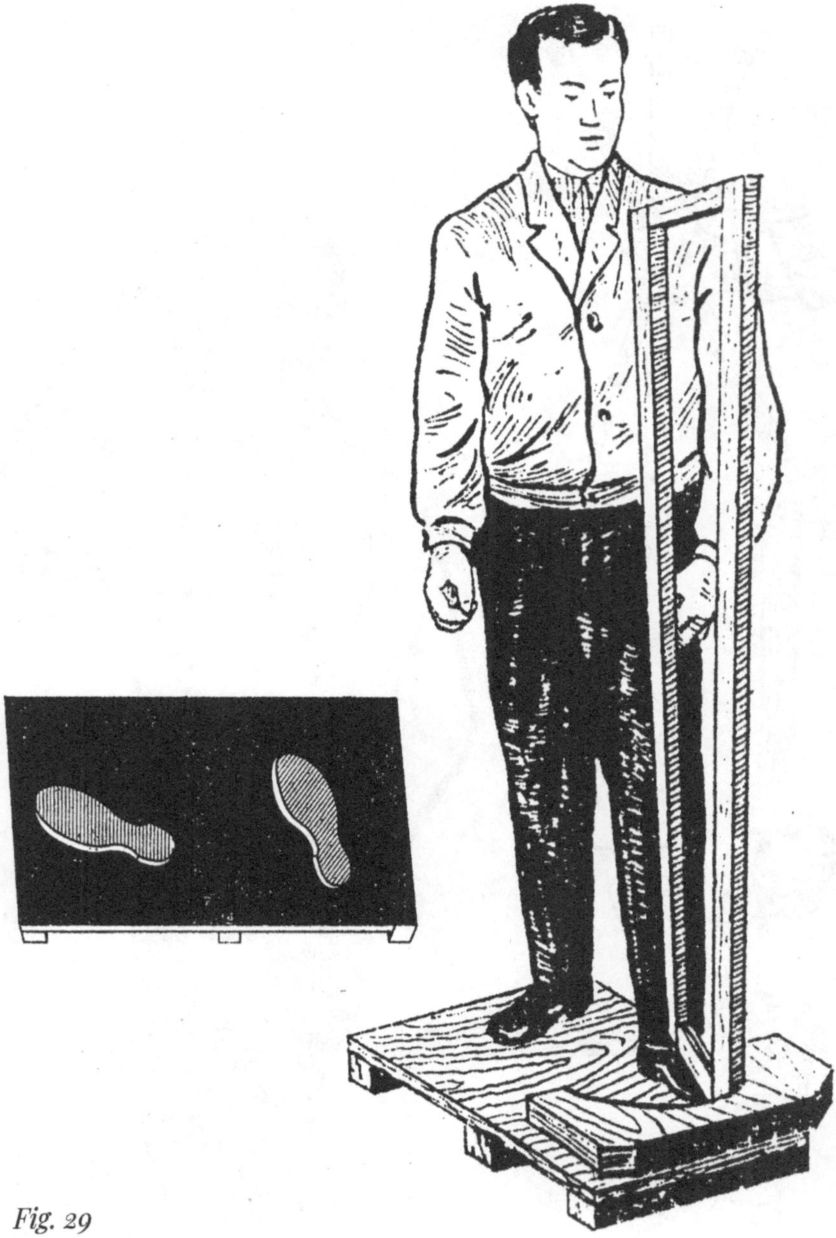

Fig. 29

Fig. 30

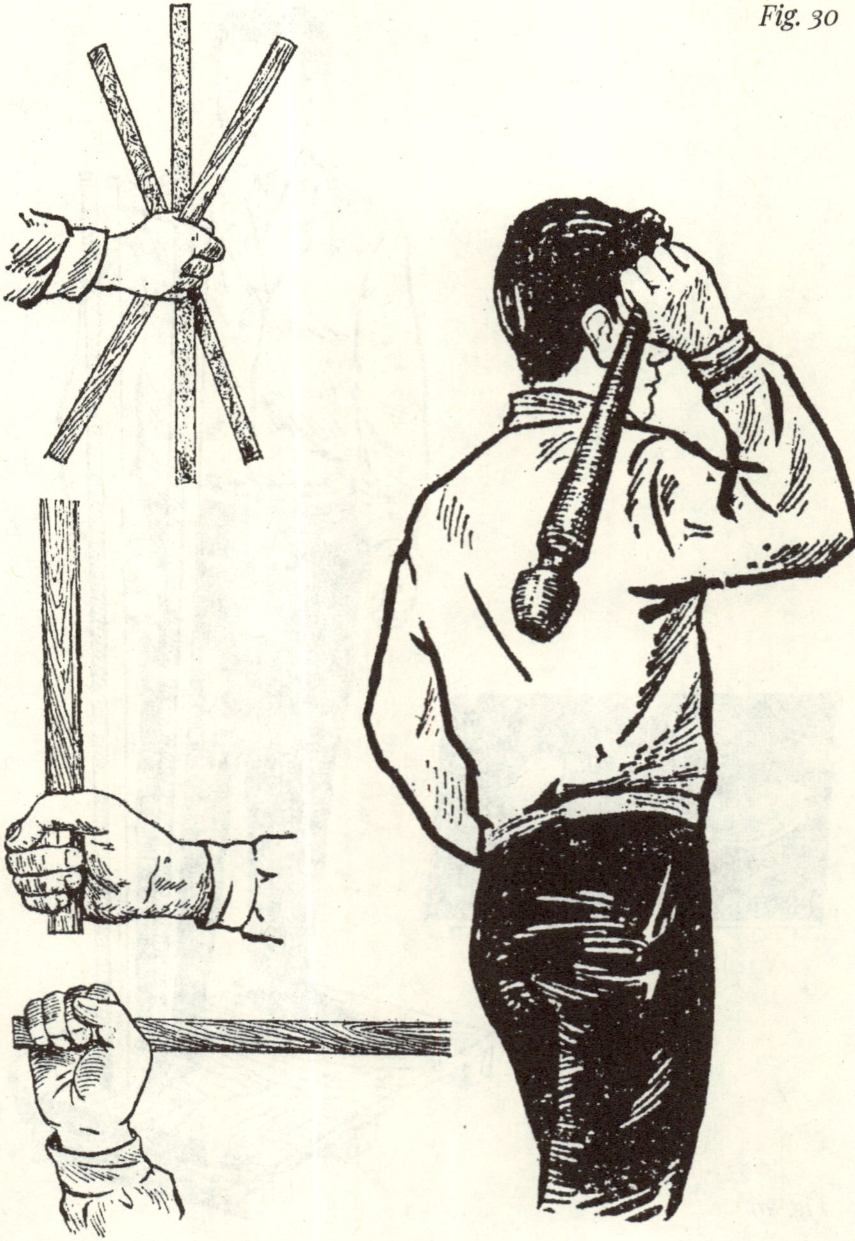

Fig. 31

according to Gastev, and in a more consistent sequence of muscular contractions. This, in turn, would create *muscle memory*, through which the "organism learns to use only specific muscles, at a specific speed and in an appropriate sequence, when working." Thanks to this muscle memory, Gastev wrote, workers could rest their muscles and supply them with oxygen while executing the movement. Not only does such a sequence provide "the most direct path to a given movement," delivering "a high-intensity blow with minimal motion," it also evidences "minimal consumption of muscular energy."[15] By routinizing these hammering motions, Gastev hoped to form *nerve-muscle memory* and achieve an economy of neural energy.

6.3 The biomechanics of movement

To establish such a routine, Gastev began by training the wrist with the help of a guide. The worker was forced to insert his arm into the guide in such a way that "the end of the forearm bone adjacent to the wrist rests in a specially shaped indentation"; a handrest kept the other hand immobile while helping to stabilize the body (Fig. 31).

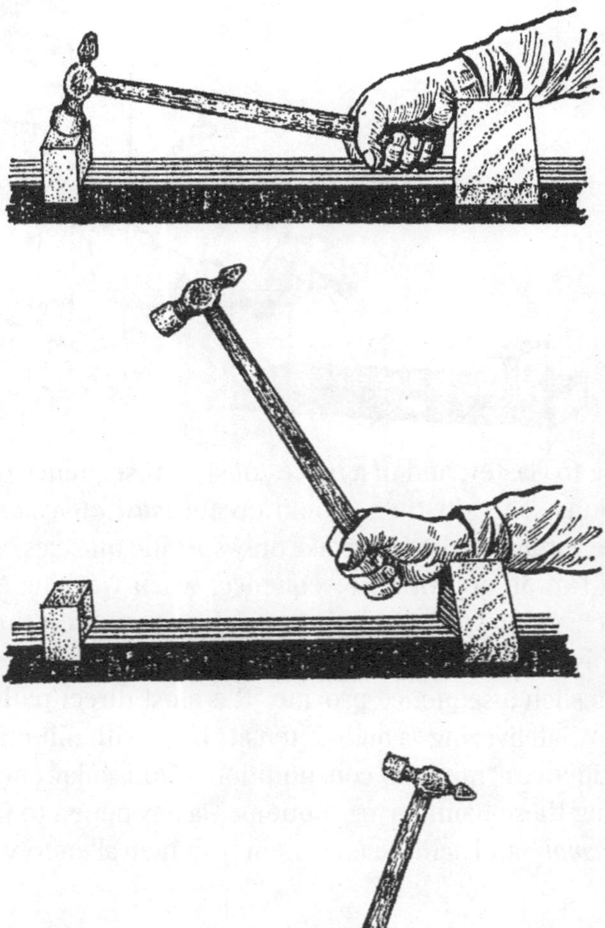

Fig. 32

After that, three positions were set (Fig. 32): "The first position to be set is the "ready" position: the wrist is moved downward until the head of the hammer contacts the anvil. Second position: the wrist is raised, lifting the hammer. Third position: the hammer is drawn back while the wrist remains raised and the three motor fingers release their grip."[16]

Whereas the second position served to train the wrist joint as a whole, with the ultimate goal of "working skillfully with small levers," it was the third and most important position in the exercise that revealed to workers the cause of their wrist fatigue. In this position, the fingers and wrist were set in motion by muscles located near the elbow, whose contraction and relaxation could be observed in "the clenching [and] opening of the fist, primarily on the inner forearm." The purpose of training, for Gastev, was to enable the worker "to use different groups of fingers in his work: now to grasp the hammer with the pivot fingers, now to set the motor fingers in motion, wrapping them around the hammer handle, but without tension." Only when the ability to work with isolated muscle groups had been attained could the necessary nerve-muscle memory be formed, "solidifying" the separate movement sequences in the wrist so that the guide would no longer be required.[17]

Building on this acquired nerve-muscle memory, Gastev then moved to the "elbow guide" (Fig. 33), which differed from the wrist guide "only in that the support for the forearm bone adjacent to the elbow is positioned at a greater height and distance."[18] The training of the elbow and its own particular nerve-muscle memory followed the same pattern, on the whole, as that of the wrist exercises: "First we do 'practice runs' with the elbow: We take the hammer in the hand and raise it slightly to strike, keeping the wrist under moderate tension. The motor fingers wrap around the hammer handle without grasping it, while the thumb and index finger act to check the resulting centrifugal force. Once the first position has been set, we raise the hammer by straightening the elbow, thereby training the

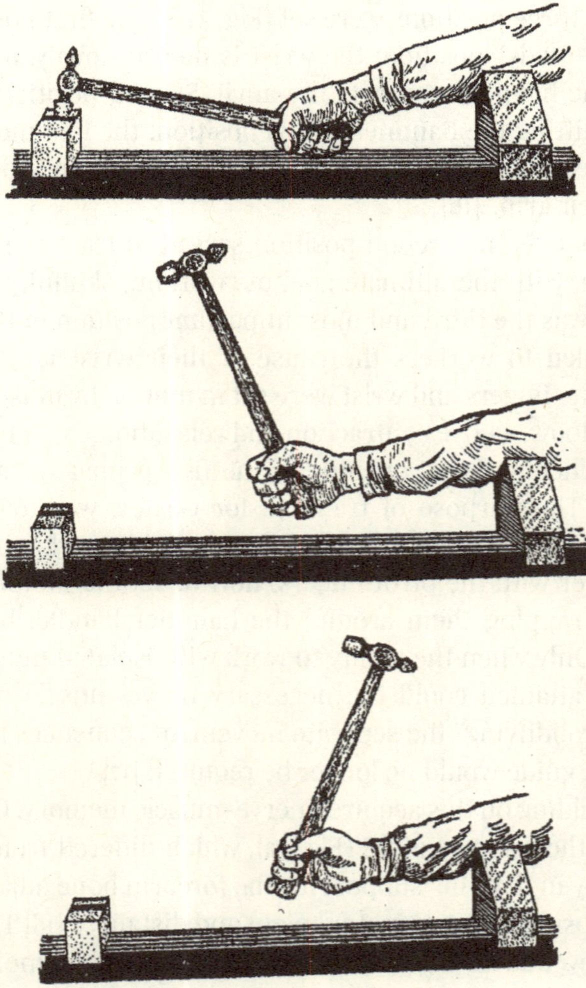

Fig. 33

biceps (raising) and triceps (lowering)."[19] After the elbow's "local nerve-muscle memory" had been trained, the wrist muscles were "activated" as well, combining maximum elevation of the elbow with maximum elevation of the wrist to produce an "integrated hammering action originating in the elbow."[20]

Fig. 34

Next came shoulder lever training, to consolidate the nerve-muscle memory of the wrist and elbow once these had been sufficiently trained. This involved a guide "resembling a crutch"(Fig. 34), permitting a vertical setting so that the shoulder and chest muscles could be incorporated into the execution of the movement as well: "To achieve a backswing on the model of the stone carver, while at the same time imparting the necessary freedom to the movement, we provide the trainee with a template [see bottom half of Figure 6]. We have borrowed the sculptor's manikin to serve as the basis of this template, using it to indicate the hammering and backswing positions of the lever as symbolized by the jointed arm."[21]

With regard to the triply interlinked nerve-muscle memory of wrist, elbow, and shoulder, Gastev noted that "increased

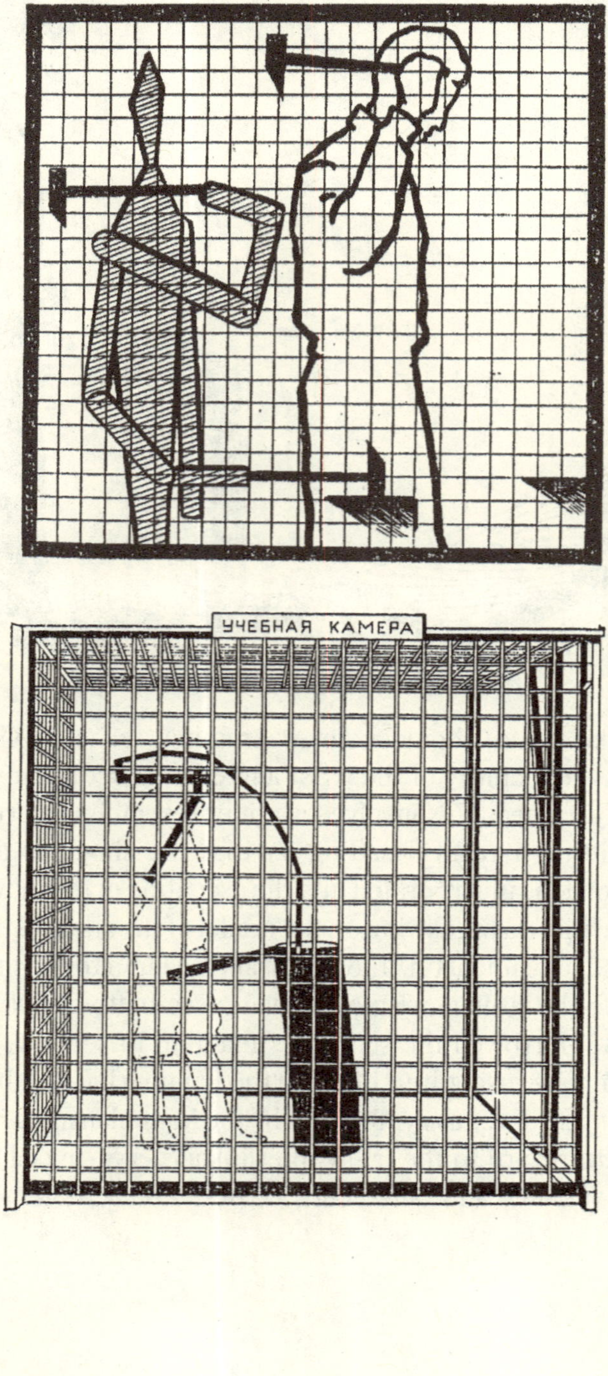

Fig. 35

demonstrative persuasiveness" could be achieved with the help of projections in what he called a "training chamber": on the wall, the trainee would see silhouettes of the arm delivering a blow with the hammer, including the backswing and the various stages of the downswing (Fig. 35).[22] By constantly increasing the demands of training in accordance with "the principle of the gradual addition of levers and activation of motors," Gastev and his colleagues at the CIT investigated the biomechanics of the hammer blow.[23] The insights thus obtained, and the dynamics thus ingrained, could then be applied to everyday life, where they would be "generally referred to as skill."[24] It was precisely this transition, from the seemingly mechanical procedure of hammering to the psychophysiological settings implied by skill, that enabled Gastev to extend the biomechanics of the hammer blow to other work processes.

6.4 Applying the method

Before the biomechanics of the hammer blow could flower into a routine hammering action in everyday life, Gastev and his colleagues added three further criteria to bolster it. *Tempo*, *precision*, and *power* were the means by which they sought to perfect the regulation of nerve-muscle memory: "This connection must be present between blows so that the organism can easily adapt to the demands of its physiological and psychological sustenance." With the help of a metronome set to sixty beats per minute, Gastev attempted to instill *tempo memory*: "We compel ... the worker to maintain a regular rhythm, reinforcing this regularity through sustained training and thereby arriving at an automatic tempo. Experience has shown that after such training, the trainee can easily switch to a different tempo, even while merely going through the motions of hammering."[25]

Achieving the perfect tempo memory setting required more than just the psychotechnical effect of a ticking metronome, however.

The exercise was also accompanied by preformulated poetic passages composed by Gastev:

> I will strike the anvil with the hammer. And first I will strike exactly sixty times a minute, without looking at the clock. Second, I will hammer so that I maintain a tempo of 120 blows in the first quarter-minute, 90 blows in the second quarter-minute, and 60 blows in the third.[26]

The same models used by Gastev to instill tempo memory were also used to train precision. By unerringly striking the target, he claimed, the worker would develop an "acute feeling for the path of the hammer." Finally, "properly maintained speed and solid precision" were joined by strength training. This involved the use of a dynamometer, which served not only "a purely physiological purpose (the enhancement of muscular activity) but also a psychological one (the imparting of confidence and purpose to the wrist)."[27] Through the proper pacing and precise application of strength, Gastev sought to achieve the "maximum quantity of work while maintaining a constant expenditure of effort."[28]

According to Gastev, this succession of settings – comprising both the construction of the hammering action and the exercises to train the worker's tempo, precision, and power – constituted a blueprint "for the learning of natural work."[29] Through the projection of an automatic hammering action onto chisel work, Gastev created a universal methodology for blacksmithing and metalworking, and he claimed that analogous sequences could also be used in "woodworking, tailoring, and breadmaking"; to Gastev, "methodical work in the field of instrumental-muscular processes" seemed to be "unlimited in its applications." And the possibility of transposing the basic instructions for these "instrumental-muscular processes" onto "mechanical work" bore this out: "This underlying analysis enabled us to get our bearings quite quickly in the gigantic, constructive world of machines. Our experience in factories, which had given us empirical knowledge of machines, granted us access to machine tools, not only in the immense variety of their construction, but also in the limitless diversity of their organization. Our systematic work with machines first took the form of meticulous analyses of the various types of machines, followed by the analysis of entire organizational classes."[30]

Armed with his "carefully worked-out instructions for instrumental-muscular processes" and the "conservatism of the manual training method" (which was fundamentally mechanical, based as it was on rigid constructive settings), Gastev took the last logical step, transitioning "to the synthetic world of production" – that is, to automated assembly. His mastery of instrumental-muscular and mechanical processes enabled him to discover "a training method for assembly" that spontaneously gave rise to "the idea of the method's universal applicability as a system of education and of organizational adaptation." His method of self-regulating, self-actuating hammering thus transcended the problem of training, becoming "a far-reaching research concept, a system of education, a system of organization, and ultimately a system of culture."[31] Skill was to be "the most important idea" in this culture, for skill, Gastev wrote, is "the art of constructing movements, an art that provides a foundation for practically infinite accomplishment and that can be worked out, from the theoretical perspective, with microscopic precision."[32]

However, while a system involving projected representations, microscopic scrutiny, and self-regulating programming did become, under Lenin, the blueprint for reshaping an entire state,[33] in the Stalin era that same method would be the undoing of its inventor: Gastev was arrested for "counterrevolutionary terrorist activities" on September 8, 1938, condemned to death on April 14, 1939, and executed by firing squad outside Moscow on the following day.

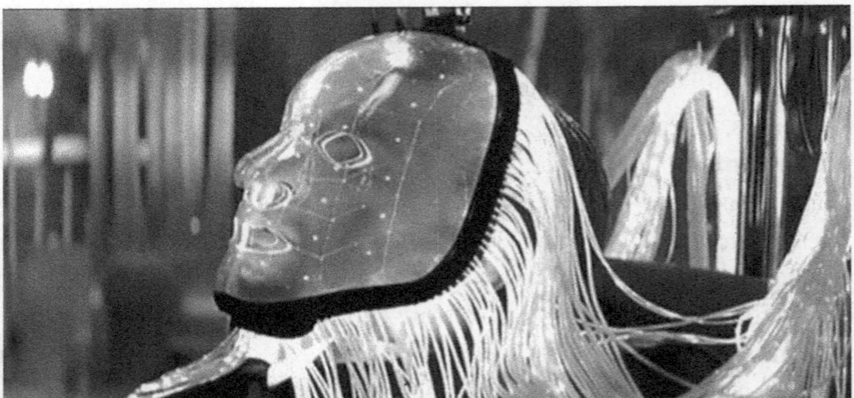

Fig. 36

7 Hypnotic states

7.1 Sleep as political metaphor

In contemporary criticism of global capitalism, sleep has awakened as a central theme. The universal claim must now be made that sleep, as a state of rest from work, has itself become the product of work. Perhaps the most prominent statement of this opinion is Jonathan Crary's 2013 book *24/7*, whose subtitle, *Late Capitalism and the Ends of Sleep*, makes its author's stance immediately clear. The combination of our round-the-clock, seven-days-a-week availability with the possibility of nonstop consumption has resulted in a 24–7 capitalism that devours every last social observance in our everyday lives not yet connected to productivity. New technological products and global networks act as a second sun that turns night into day.

A technological sun that brings not only illumination, but also military power, is a central element in the 2002 James Bond movie *Die Another Day*. In the film, Bond's North Korean adversary Colonel Moon undergoes gene therapy to change his looks and identity. One side effect of this treatment is permanent insomnia. While Gustav Graves, as Moon is now called, brags about how much more he can accomplish now that he no longer needs sleep – "plenty of time to sleep when you're dead," he says to Bond – he actually feels quite tortured by his inability to sleep and tries to escape it with the help of a "dream machine" (Fig. 36). The villain is thus trapped between two technological developments – the artificial sun, called Icarus, and the dream machine – both of which play a part in his downfall.

Although Crary does not mention *Die Another Day* in his Marxist-influenced analysis, he returns again and again to the argument that creative use of technological tools is essential for survival in the 24–7 society, and that such creative use is only possible in a socialist context. The Soviet authorities simply failed to take advantage of their opportunity, says Crary: "Lenin, Trotsky and their cohort made use of every communications technology at hand in 1917, but they never elevated them to privileged and sacrosanct determinants of an entire constellation of historical events, as some cyberactivists have done in extolling the role of social media in recent political movements and uprisings."[1] The following is intended to show that Crary is absolutely wrong on this point.

7.2 A radio-controlled world

At the dawn of Soviet rule, after the October Revolution, it was widely believed that mental energy was similar to electromagnetic energy, and that it was only a matter of time until Communist society would no longer need wires to hear the voice of Moscow.[2] The Russian futurist Velimir Khlebnikov conjured this vision of a radio-controlled world in his technological fantasies of *radio budushchego*, the radio of the future: "Doctors today can treat patients long-distance, through hypnotic suggestion. Radio in the future will be able to act also as a doctor, healing patients without medicine."[3] Such visions – of which we shall see more later – were clearly consonant with the new regime's plan to attain Communism through the multiplication of Soviet power and the electrification of the whole country.

Another milestone toward the realization of these visions was Hans Berger's invention of the electroencephalograph (EEG) in 1924 (Fig. 37). This device made it possible to record the physical energy of the brain – "to watch the brain thinking," as it were.[4] It also made it possible to document the different stages of sleep, which

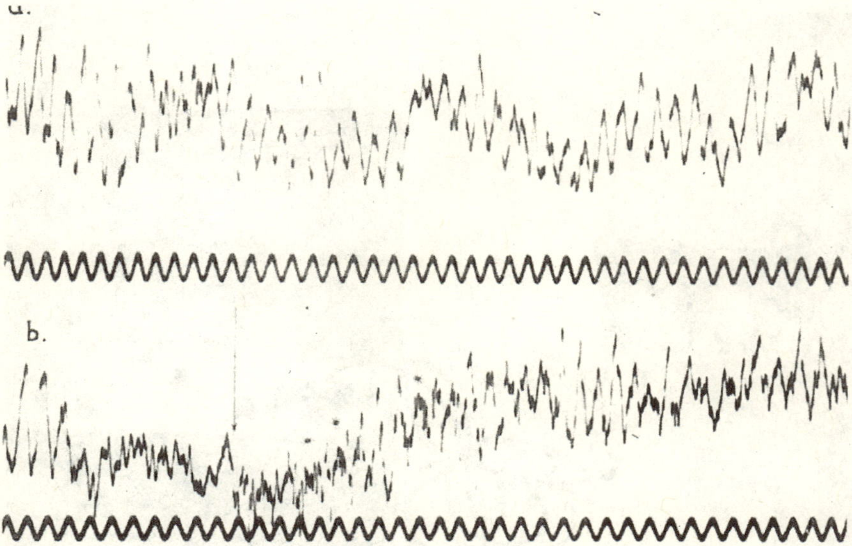

Fig. 37

had already been the subject of various physiological studies. Ivan Pavlov, for example, had come to view sleep as a generalized form of the inhibition of reflexes, a process that could also be observed during the normal waking state: “Inhibition is partial sleep, or sleep distributed in localized parts, forced into narrow limits; true sleep is a diffused and continuous inhibition of the whole of the [cerebral] hemispheres.”[5]

Pavlov found that the brain passed through a number of discrete states in transitioning from wakefulness to sleep: “the equalization state when in contrast to the wakeful state all stimuli, irrespective of their intensity, act with an absolutely equal force; the paradoxical state, when only the weak stimuli act, or when the strong stimuli act, too, but produce a barely noticeable effect; and finally, the ultra-paradoxical state when only the previously elaborated inhibitory agents produce a positive effect – a state followed by complete inhibition.”[6] How quickly this state of “complete

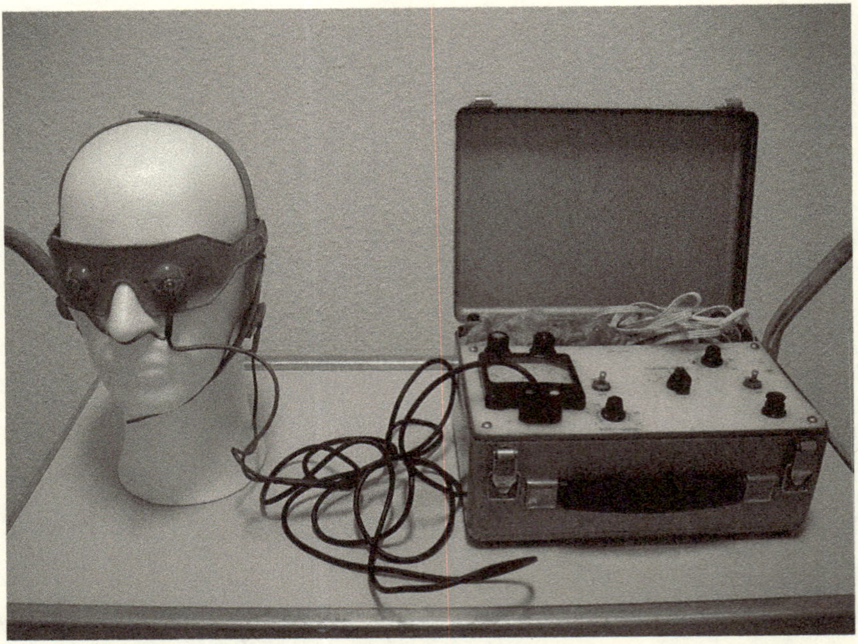

Fig. 38

inhibition" takes hold depends, according to Pavlov, on external conditions, the types of cortical functions involved, and the state of the central nervous system at the time.

Sleep, for Pavlov, appeared to be a kind of protective reaction by the organism, and therefore the best therapy for pathological conditions of the nervous system. His work in this area led to the concept of "protective therapy," which sought not only to preserve the hypnotic state, but to intensify it to a heightened state of "sleep inhibition."[7] Building on these theories, researchers in the late 1940s began to explore the possibility of using electricity to artificially induce or intensify a state of protective inhibition. Pavlov had noted that "three different types of external stimuli lead to an inhibitory state of the cortex, namely, very weak stimuli, very strong

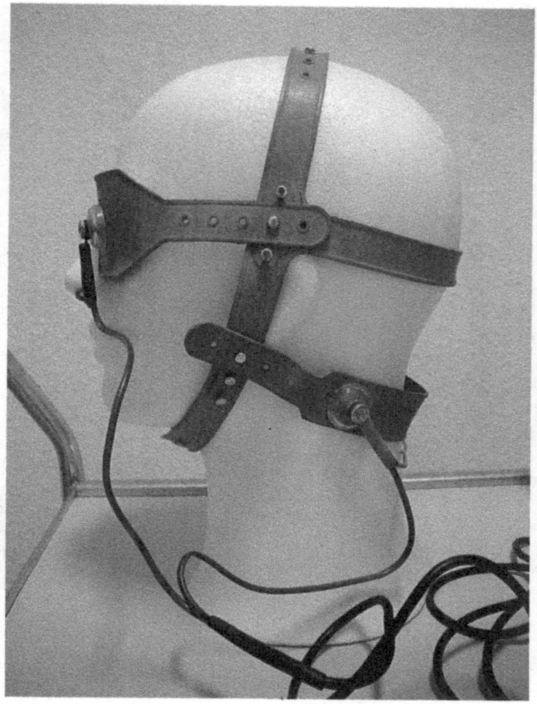

Fig. 39

stimuli, and unusual stimuli."[8] In studying the effects of the very weak stimuli, the Soviet psychiatrist Vasily Alekseyevich Gilyarovsky and his team learned how to produce a sleeping or sleeplike state, which they envisioned serving as a prosthetic optimization for the pathologically altered brain. This phenomenon came to be known as "electrosleep" (Fig. 38).

To prepare his subjects, Gilyarovsky placed electrodes over each eye and on the back of the neck, reasoning that the current would enter the skull by way of the eye socket (anode), spread throughout the brain tissue via the blood vessels and cerebral ventricles, and then exit at the neck (cathode) (Fig. 39). He then applied a very weak (0.01-milliampere) square-wave pulsed current at a frequency of 1–10 hertz, with a pulse width of 0.2 milliseconds.

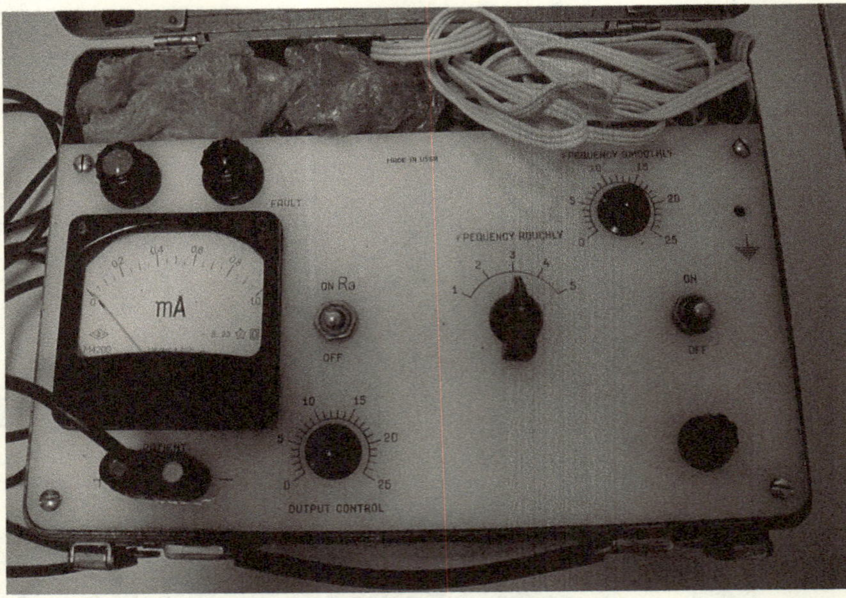

Fig. 40

(Interestingly, Gilyarovsky considered it necessary that the subject feel the electricity as a pleasant tingling.) It is precisely these low levels that distinguish electrosleep from electroanesthesia, which employs a current of 40 milliamperes at a voltage of 20 volts and a frequency of 100–200 hertz – levels that Gilyarovsky classed among the "strong stimuli" (Fig. 40).

In Gilyarovsky's view, the potential applications of his optimized dream machine extended far beyond the treatment of insomnia and other sleep disorders. And indeed, a number of physicians, from the Eastern Bloc and beyond, reported success in using electrosleep to treat a variety of illnesses, including mental disorders and neuroses, depression and schizophrenia, high and low blood pressure, impotence, and other generalized and localized circulatory disorders. One Western European champion

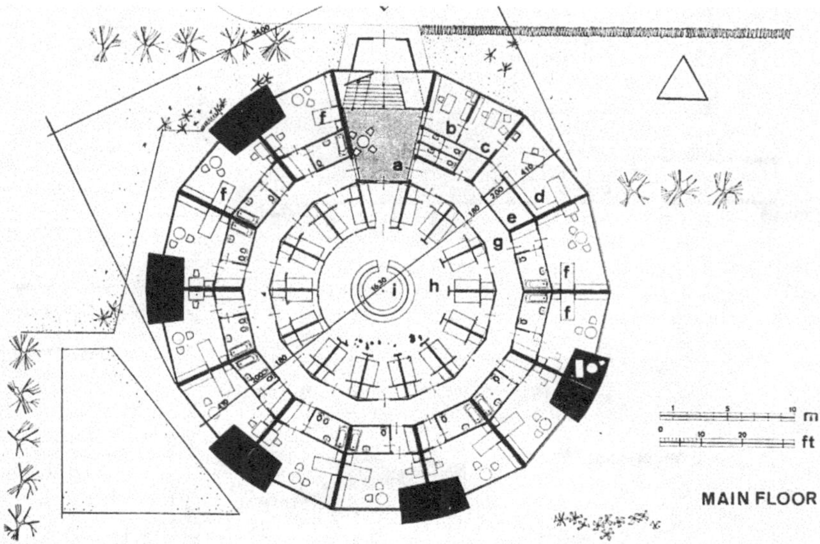

Ground plan of the main floor of the therapy centre; from the centre outward: 1st ring: central control, 2nd ring: treatment cells, 3rd ring: apartments.

Fig. 41a

of electrosleep, the Austrian psychotherapist Franz Wageneder, even claimed to have successfully treated a heroin addict, noting that "the suggestive effect of [sleep therapy] is no greater than that inherent to any medical activity. No damage was observed from the minimal current flowing through the brain. With proper diagnosis and careful treatment, the patient has a good chance of recovery. Whether such recovery or healing is the result of suggestion or of the electrical current alone may be of great importance to the scientist, but for the patient it is doubtless completely immaterial."[9]

It was also Wageneder who, in 1965, organized the first international conference on electrosleep and electroanesthesia in Graz, where he proposed to build a center for electrosleep therapy and research. Regarding the floor plan of this surveillance complex

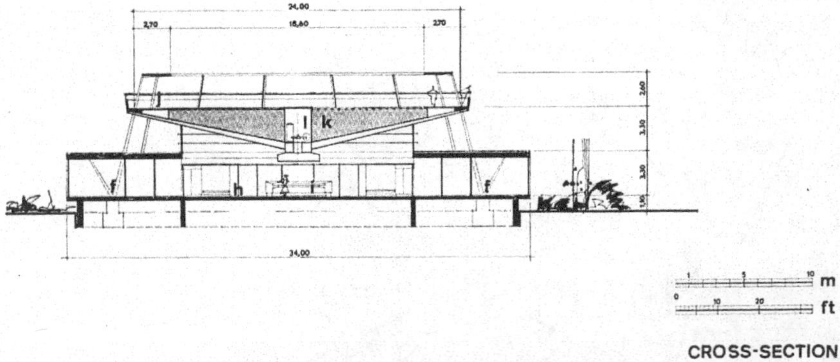

Cross section of the therapy centre.

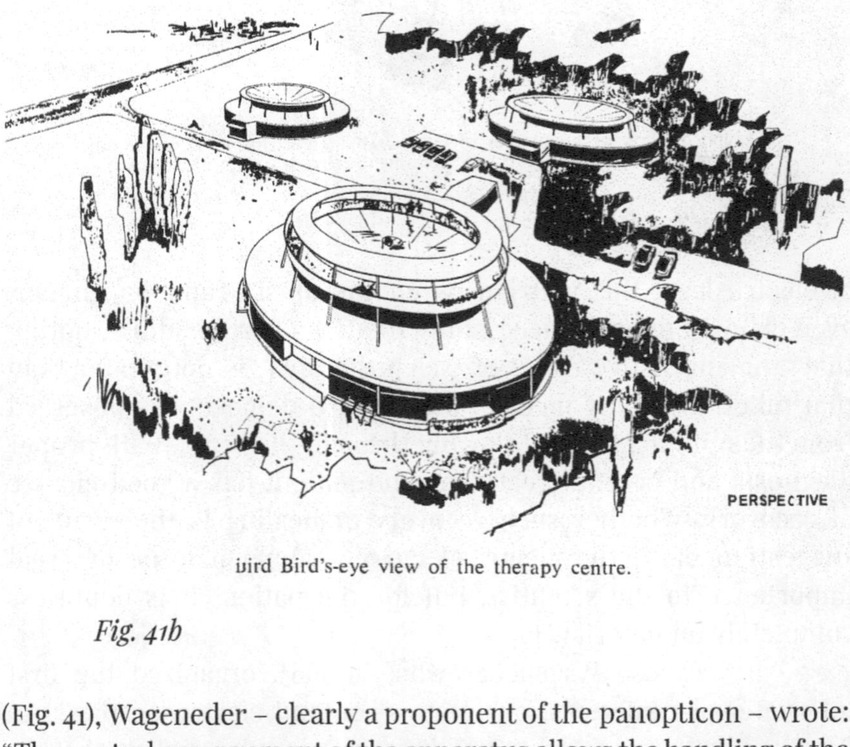

uird Bird's-eye view of the therapy centre.

Fig. 41b

(Fig. 41), Wageneder – clearly a proponent of the panopticon – wrote: "The central arrangement of the apparatus allows the handling of the equipment by a single person, who has the patient in full view."[10]

Fig. 42

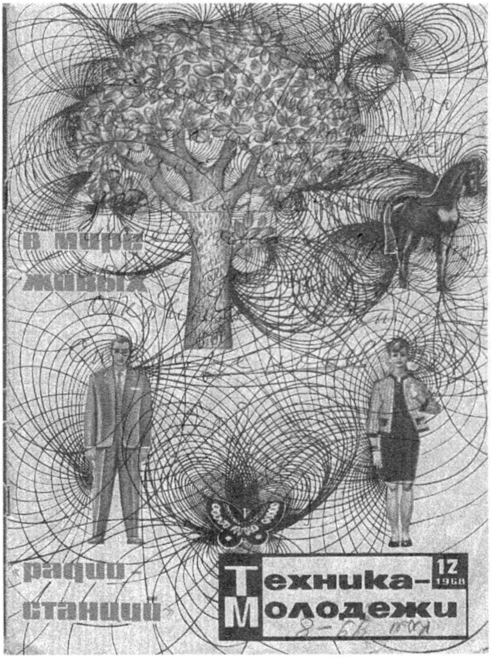

7.3 The aurathrone

These discoveries and inventions gave rise to further dreams and visions. "Imagine a medical center in the near future," began Pavel Gulyaev's 1968 article "Biologicheskaya svyaz' deystvuyet" (Biological communication activated). The vision continued: "A patient comes into the office. Machines record electro-auragrams of his brain, heart, nerves, muscles, and internal organs, then transmit the information to an electronic diagnostic machine that diagnoses the illness and prescribes the appropriate treatment. All this happens in a matter of seconds; the patient does not even have to undress."[11]

Gulyaev's article appeared in the Soviet popular science magazine *Tekhnika-molodezhi* (Youth technology), in an issue entitled "V mire zhivykh radiostantsiy" (In the world of living radio stations) (Fig. 42). In it, scientists from the Laboratory of Physiological

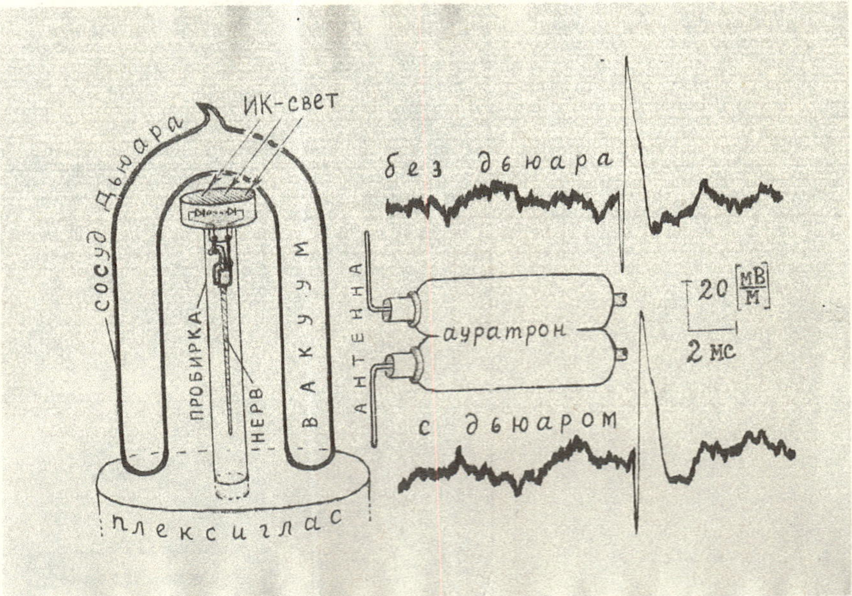

Fig. 43

Cybernetics, which Gulyaev directed, reported on twenty years of research, describing what they considered to be a phenomenal result: the use of an “aurathrone” to measure the electrical field of the human nervous system at a distance of 25 centimeters (Fig. 43): “This field only exists for a thousandth of a second (the time it takes the impulse to travel along the nerve). If we consider that our body contains more than four million nerve pathways, and that the activity of the impulses is constantly changing, we can imagine just how complex the whole nervous system of a *Homo sapiens* actually is.”[12]

The scientists working under Gulyaev saw their experiments as confirmation of prevailing ideas about brain waves and telepathy. Their experiments at the Laboratory for Physiological Cybernetics provided the scientific basis for hypothesizing a biomagnetic medium, which Gulyaev named *psichon*. In addition to the readings

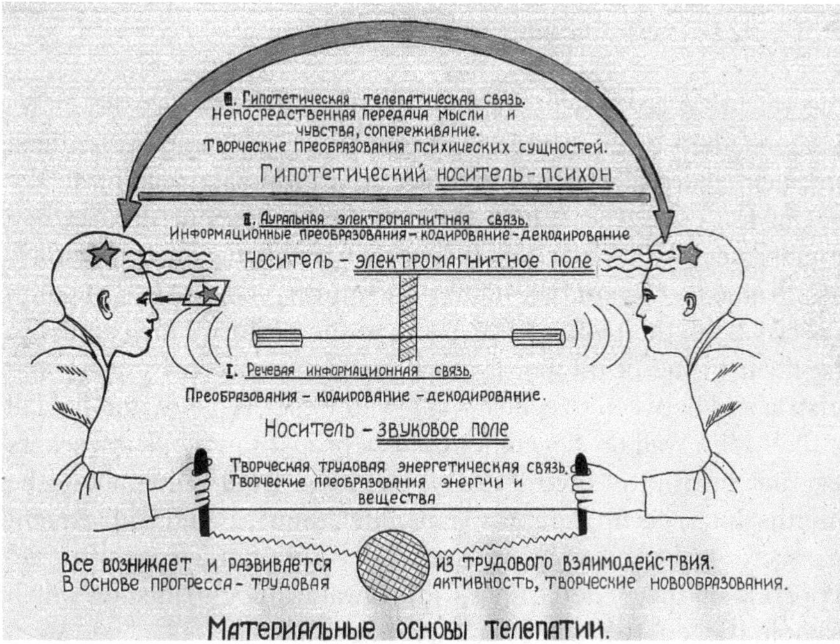

Fig. 44

they took, there is also a drawing by Gulyaev (Fig. 44) that shows this medium's mediating qualities materializing in a feedback loop between *control over media* and *control by media*. We are clearly looking at a transfer of knowledge via thought, patterned on physical transmission technologies, which inscribes itself on the receiving end as an immediate effect; that is, it becomes reality. The stars in place of brains remind us that the potential for thought transference in this cybernetic system is very much politically instrumentalized – an approach that legitimizes censorship and control via what is claimed to be scientific knowledge. In its medical aspect, this medium would reach its zenith just as the Soviet Union was at its nadir, when the hope was that people skeptical of the system would be "healed" by "regenerating powers."

7.4 Let your thoughts run free

The year that began with George Bush taking office as the forty-first president of the United States would become one of the most turbulent years of the twentieth century, ultimately leading to the end of the Cold War. A look through the archives of the German broadcasters ARD and ZDF shows that reporting on the historic events of 1989 delivered the highest TV ratings recorded to that point. Newscasts on the political upheavals in the Eastern Bloc countries, the dismantling of the border fortifications between Hungary and Austria and between Czechoslovakia and West Germany, and the fall of the Berlin Wall on November 9, 1989, brought millions of viewers together in front of their TV sets. The news from China about the months-long occupation of Tiananmen Square and subsequent massacre provoked viewers' outrage – in marked contrast to reporting on the Soviet army's withdrawal from Afghanistan, which brought the ten-year Soviet-Afghan War to an end.

While these reports were traveling around the entire world and reshaping the televisual landscape, a different picture prevailed in the still-extant Soviet Union. Although the events mentioned above also appeared in news reports on the state television network's Channel One, what captured viewers' attention, in what were then still fifteen united republics, was a program broadcast at 8:30 p.m. that October, right after the evening news.

"Relax, let your thoughts run free": this was one of the first sentences spoken by Anatoly Kashpirovsky to his audience, the entire Soviet Union.[13] Before this session Kashpirovsky, a trained physician, had worked for twenty-five years as a psychotherapist in a psychiatric hospital, spending the two years immediately preceding his television debut as the psychotherapist for the Soviet national weightlifting team. After the 1988 Olympics in Seoul – where the USSR dominated, winning 132 medals, including six golds for weightlifting – the popularity of Kashpirovsky's psychic adjustments had spread far beyond the sporting world. Now the techniques he had successfully used on athletes would soothe a country perturbed by change – treating it, healing it, and above all preparing it for the new goals of the Soviet Union against a background of impending change. It had become obvious that neither the policies of reform implemented thus far nor the subsequent restructuring of the system, with its slogans of glasnost and perestroika, had had any convincing effect. The population seemed to be slowly awakening from some kind of trance, realizing what had really been happening during the last years of the regime and seeing how far they were from Western standards of living and the economic power of the global leaders. Now a new and apparently "healing" power (rather than an unambiguously political one) was to take the place of individual passivity as the perpetuator of this trancelike state.

The first of Kashpirovsky's six broadcasts took place on October 9, 1989. While seventy thousand people were demonstrating in Leipzig, chanting "We are the people" in the first mass demonstration against the East German regime since 1953, in the land of perestroika, millions of people were spending the evening sitting in front of their televisions, allowing a "miracle worker" to prepare them for the changes to come: "You can keep your eyes open for a while. Look around at the environment you are in. There should not be any sharp objects or open flames nearby. Your body should be in a stable position. If anyone is seriously ill – if you suffer from epilepsy, for example – please do not participate in our séance, just switch off your TV."[14]

While the first shot of Kashpirovsky's twenty-minute teleséance (Fig. 45) shows the hypnotist in close-up as he speaks to the audience, a fade to the second shot (Fig. 46) reveals the scene of the event. Kashpirovsky can be seen on the stage at the front of an auditorium, from which he delivers his instructions, placing his audience in a trance. The iconography of the third and final shot (Fig. 47) makes the political import of the session quite clear: as the

Fig. 45

Fig. 46

Fig. 47

camera pans across the room, followed by the gaze of the viewers sitting in front of their TV sets, the hypnotist's head is superimposed on the auditorium. Floating, to anodyne effect, above all who see and hear it, this head is literally sublime.

The final session of this séance was broadcast on Channel One on Friday, November 10, 1989. After watching a brief report on the opening of the Berlin Wall the night before, viewers remained seated in front of their televisions – to recover from the shocking news and be healed by dreams.

7.5 Systems crash

In this interference field between mediations and the symbolic, systematic, and rhetorical ways in which they organize data and information, the specific mode of representation of Soviet media historiography is unmasked: formed in a coupling of physical and nonphysical technologies, it would go on to heat up the bodies of the Cold War. At the end of that war of two systems, in which representations of public opinion played a strategic role, the people on one side let themselves be entranced by a televisual séance, a public faith healing through which the Soviet system made a final attempt to bind its people's secret thoughts to itself and commit public existence to visions not yet extinguished.

This institutionalization of sleep, and of the dreams directly associated with it, problematizes Crary's analysis of late capitalism. An image not of the decline of the socialist system as outlined above, but rather of the incipient collapse of 24–7 capitalism, already existed in 1926, created by the Soviet science fiction writer Alexander Belyaev. His short story "Chelovek, kotoryy ne spit" (The man who does not sleep) is about the Soviet scientist Wagner and his pharmaceutical discoveries. After publishing his findings in the Soviet Union and announcing that, having conquered sleep and thrown away his bed (which was just a symbol of the hospital), he can now do research twenty-four hours a day, he is kidnapped by Diktator, an organization of German radicals. The group's leaders trick Wagner into producing pills for the masses so that people can be permanently active.

Work and revelry, making and spending money, thus become the Germans' only goals in life, and Diktator becomes an empire. Once Wagner finds out what is really going on, however, he plans his escape and the collapse of the system: he has the next batch of pills manufactured without the antitoxin that counteracts the accumulation of sleep-inducing toxins in the body, and the entire population of Germany falls asleep. Wagner manages to escape and discovers that he was being held captive the whole time in Berlin. Wandering the streets of the German capital, which are filled with sleeping, snoring people, he finds his way to the airport and flies back to Moscow, back to the Soviet Union.[15]

If we consider this fiction of capitalist exhaustion with one eye on the aforementioned "sacrosanct determinants" of the Soviet system, it should be clear that the collapse of a political system or orientation, undoubtedly a most significant political event, is also inevitable. In this destiny, however, collective dreams, whether induced by pharmaceuticals or by the media, are also accompanied by political hallucinations. And it is precisely those hallucinations that bring about the collapse of political coordinate systems that had seemed stable just moments before.

Acknowledgments

Chapter 1

[1] Radom House Unabridged Dictionary, 2nd Edition (1987), S. 1917

Chapter 2

[1] Evgeny Trubetskoy, *Dva mira v drevne-russkoy ikonopisi* (Moscow: Mamontova, 1916), 3; italics in the original. The word *otkrytie*, translated here as "unveiling," can also signify revelation, opening, or discovery. (All translations from Russian are provided by the author and translator of this essay unless otherwise noted.)

[2] Quoted in Y. A. Rusakov, "Matisse in Russia in the Autumn of 1911," trans. John E. Bowlt, *The Burlington Magazine*, no. 866 (May 1975): 288. See also Y. V. Bruk and L. I. Iovleva, *Gosudarstvennaya Tret'yakovskaya galereya*, vol. 1, *Drevnerusskoye iskusstvo X–nachala XV veka* (Moscow: Krasnaya ploshchad', 1995), as well as Nikolai Punin, "Puti sovremennogo iskusstva i russkaya ikonopis," *Apollon* 5, no. 9 (November 1913): 52–64.

[3] Giorgio Agamben, *Profanations*, trans. Jeff Fort (New York: Zone Books, 2007), 83. See also Giorgio Agamben, *Homo Sacer: Sovereign Power and Bare Life*, trans. Daniel Heller-Roazen (Stanford: Stanford University Press, 1998), 45–68.

[4] Pavel Muratov, "Vystavka drevne-russkogo iskusstva v Moskve," pt. 1, *Starye gody*, April 1913, 31. See also Pavel Muratov et al., *Vystavka drevne-russkogo iskusstva, ustroyennaya v 1913 godu v oznamenovaniye chestvovaniye 300-letiye tsarstvovaniye*

Doma Romanovykh (Moscow: Imperatorskiy Moskovskiy Arkheologicheskiy Institut imeni Imperatora Nikolaya II, 1913).

[5] Ibid.

[6] Trubetskoy, *Dva mira*, 3.

[7] There is also a type of icon cover that merely frames the edges of the icon, known as a *basma* (border). See Gabriele von Horn, *Neues Wörterbuch zur Ikonenkunst* (Neckenmarkt: NovumPro, 2010), 83.

[8] See for example Bernhard Bornheim, *Ikonen* (Augsburg: Battenberg, 1990), 156.

[9] A characteristic example is the late-twelfth-century account of Gervase of Tilbury, who described an image of Christ that was kept among the Church's relics in Rome. Gervase of Tilbury, *Otia Imperialia: Recreation for an Emperor*, ed. and trans. S. E. Banks and J. W. Binns (Oxford: Clarendon, 2002), 604–07.

[10] See for example Ernst Günther Grimme, *Goldschmiedekunst im Mittelalter. Form und Bedeutung des Reliquiars von 800–1500* (Cologne: DuMont Schauberg, 1972).

[11] Bornheim, *Ikonen*, 156.

[12] Katherine Kennedy, *The Crucifix: An Outline Sketch of Its History* (London: Mowbray, 1917), 33. See also Josef Wohlmuth, ed., *Streit um das Bild. Das Zweite Konzil von Nizäa (787) in ökumenischer Perspektive* (Bonn: Bouvier, 1989).

[13] On the numinous, see Rudolf Otto, *Das Heilige. Über das Irrationale in der Idee des Göttlichen und sein Verhältnis zum Rationalen* (Breslau: Trewendt und Granier, 1920), 5–7.

[14] See: Marcel Mauss, *The Gift: The Form and Reason for Exchange in Archaic Societies*, trans. W. D. Halls (Abingdon: Routledge Classics, 2002); Marcel Hénaff, *The Price of Truth: Gift, Money, and Philosophy*, trans. Jean-Louis Morhange and Anne-Marie Feenberg-Dibon (Stanford: Stanford University Press, 2010); Sigmund Freud, *Totem and Taboo: Some Points of Agreement between the Mental Lives of Savages and Neurotics*, trans. James Strachey (New York: Norton, 1962); and Otto, *Das Heilige*, 14–21.

[15] Georges Didi-Huberman, *La ressemblance par contact. Archéologie, anachronisme et modernité de l'empreinte* (Paris: Minuit, 2008), 81. If the offering is accompanied by direct "contact" with the sacred, then "one of the simplest forms of profanation" has taken place (Agamben, *Profanations*, 74).

[16] Ukase of Peter the Great on offerings, January 21, 1772, F. 270, op. 1, no. 100, l. 59, Archive of the Saint Petersburg Institute of History.

[17] Jean-Luc Nancy, *The Ground of the Image*, trans. Jeff Fort (New York: Fordham University Press, 2005), 1.

[18] See also Richard S. Wortman, *Scenarios of Power. Myth and Ceremony in Russian Monarchy*, vol. 1 , *From Peter the Great to the Death of Nicholas I* (Princeton: Princeton University Press, 1995), 156.

[19] Oleg Tarasov, "The Russian Icon and the Culture of the Modern: The Renaissance of Popular Icon Painting in the Reign of Nicolas II," *Experiment* 7 (2001): 73–101.

[20] See also Richard S. Wortman, *Scenarios of Power. Myth and Ceremony in Russian Monarchy*, vol. 2, *From Alexander II to the Abdication of Nicholas II* (Princeton: Princeton University Press, 2000).

[21] Trubetskoy, *Dva mira*, 3.

[22] On this subject, see: Nikolai Punin, "Vystavka drevne-russkogo iskusstva v Moskva," pt. 2, *Apollon* 5, no. 5 (May 1913): 39–42; Alexandre Benois, "Khudozhestvennaya pis'ma. Ikony i novoye iskusstvo," *Rech'*, April 5, 1913, 4; Yakov Bruk, *Zhivoye naslediye. Besedy o drevnerusskoy zhivopisi* (Moscow: Iskusstvo, 1970); Hans Belting, *Likeness and Presence: A History of the Image before the Era of Art*, trans. Edmund Jephcott (Chicago: University of Chicago Press, 1994); and Verena Krieger, *Von der Ikone zur Utopie: Kunstkonzepte der russischen Avantgarde* (Cologne: Böhlau, 1998).

[23] See Hartmut Böhme, "Der Tastsinn im Gefüge der Sinne. Anthropologische und historische Ansichten vorsprachlicher Aisthesis," in *Tasten*, ed. Kunst- und Ausstellungshalle der

Bundesrepublik Deutschland (Göttingen: Steidl, 1996), 186.
[24] Trubetskoy, *Dva mira*, 3–4.
[25] Ibid., 4.
[26] Walter Benjamin, "On Language as Such and on the Language of Man," trans. Edmund Jephcott, in *Selected Writings*, vol. 1, 1913–1926, ed. Marcus Bullock and Michael W. Jennings (Cambridge, MA: Belknap, 1996), 62–74.
[27] Kazimir Malevich, letter to Mikhail Gershenzon, March 20, 1920, quoted in Yevgenia Petrova, "Malevich's Suprematism and Religion," in *Kazimir Malevich: Suprematism*, ed. Matthew Drutt (New York: Guggenheim Museum, 2003), 91.
[28] The publication of the first annotated edition of Malevich's collected writings has played a critical role in recent research: Kazimir Malevich, *Sobraniye sochineniy v pyati tomakh*, 5 vols., (Moscow: Gileya, 1995–2004).
[29] Alexandre Benois, "Poslednyaya futuristicheskaya vystavka," *Rech'*, January 9, 1916, 3.
[30] Ibid.
[31] Kazimir Malevich, *Gott ist nicht gestürzt! Schriften zu Kunst, Kirche, Fabrik*, ed. Aage A. Hansen-Löve, trans. Thomas Kleinbub and Aage A. Hansen-Löve (Munich: Hanser, 2004), 311.
[32] Wladimir Velminski, *Diagnose: Krim. Kunst und Gewandheit der Politik. Zu Besuch bei russischen Künstlern im Ausland* (Berlin: Merve, 2015), 142.
[33] Andy Warhol, *The Philosophy of Andy Warhol: From A to B and Back Again* (New York: Harcourt, 1975), 100–101.
[34] Velminski, *Diagnose: Krim*, 149.
[35] Ibid.

Chapter 3

[1] Carl Leonhard Gottlieb Ehler, letter to Leonhard Euler, March

9, 1736, Archive of the Russian Academy of Sciences, Saint Petersburg, f. 1, op. 3, no. 21, 33–36.

[2] Ibid., 37.

[3] Leonhard Euler, letter to Giovanni Jacobo Marinoni, March 13, 1736, Archive of the Russian Academy of Sciences, Saint Petersburg, f. 1, op. 3, no. 22, 18.

[4] Ibid.

[5] Ibid.

[6] Leonhard Euler, letter to Carl Leonhard Gottlieb Ehler, April 3, 1736, Archive of the Russian Academy of Sciences, Saint Petersburg, f. 1, op. 3, no. 22, 33–41(r).

[7] Leonhard Euler, "Solutio Problematis ad Geometriam Situs Pertinentis," in *Graph Theory 1736–1936*, ed. Norman L. Biggs, E. Keith Lloyd, and Robin J. Wilson (Oxford: Clarendon Press, 1998), 3. Originally published in Latin in *Commentarii Academiae Scientiarum Imperialis Petropolitanae* 8 (1736): 128–40.

[8] Ibid., 3.

[9] Euler, letter to Ehler, 37.

[10] Euler, "Solutio Problematis," 3–4.

[11] Ibid., 4.

[12] Ibid.

[13] Cf. Friedrich Kittler, "Die Stadt ist ein Medium," in *Mythos Metropole*, ed. Gotthard Fuchs, Bernhard Moltmann, and Walter Prigge (Frankfurt: Suhrkamp, 1995), 228–44.

[14] Euler, "Solutio Problematis," 4.

[15] Ibid.

[16] Ibid., 5.

[17] Ibid.

[18] Ibid., 6.

[19] Ibid., 7.

[20] Ibid.

[21] Ibid. The lowercase letters between the capital letters represent the bridges crossed.

[22] Euler, letter to Marinoni, 18.

[23] Euler, "Solutio Problematis," 8.

Chapter 4

[1] Michael Michalak, *Das homöopathische Arzneimittel. Von den Anfängen zur industriellen Fertigstellung* (Stuttgart: Wissenschaftliche Verlagsgesellschaft, 1991), 12–17.

[2] Ibid., 28.

[3] Ibid., 28–72.

[4] Semën Korsakov, "Beschreibung eines neuen Forschungsverfahrens mittels Maschinen zum Vergleich von Ideen," in *Semën Karsakov. Ideenmaschine. Von der Homöopathie zum Computer*, ed. Wladimir Velminski and Wolfgang Ernst (Berlin: Kadmos, 2008), 60.

[5] For a discussion of all five of Korsakov's "intellectual machines," see ibid., 59–80.

[6] Ibid., 51.

[7] First published in Dresden in 1810 as *Organon der rationellen Heilkunde* (*Organon of the Rational Art of Healing*), in subsequent editions the book was renamed *Organon der Heilkunst* (*Organon of Medicine*, or *Organon of the Healing Art*).

[8] Robert Jütte highlights this significant aspect of Hahnemann's scholarly background (which is also the location of his discovery of the doctrine of similarity) in *Geschichte der Alternativen Medizin. Von der Volksmedizin zu den unkonventionellen Therapien von Heute* (Munich: Beck, 1996), 179–80.

[9] Samuel Hahnemann, *Organon of Medicine*, 5th ed., trans. R. E. Dudgeon (Philadelphia: Boericke & Tafel, 1906), 98n1.

[10] He states as much in the very first sentence of his paper: "Man thinks mechanically, and his actions are executed mechanically." Korsakov, "Beschreibung," 59.

[11] Cf. Jacques Lacan, "The Function and Field of Speech and

Language in Psychoanalysis," in *Écrits: The First Complete Edition in English*, trans. Bruce Fink (New York: Norton, 1996), 197–268.

[12] Korsakov, "Beschreibung," 59.

[13] Ibid., 64.

[14] See for example Sebastian Klotz, "Ars combinatoria oder 'Musik ohne Kopfzerbrechen'. Kalküle des Musikalischen von Kircher bis Kirnberger," *Musiktheorie* 14, no. 3 (1999): 231–45; as well as Stefan Rieger: *Speichern/Merken. Die künstlichen Intelligenzen des Barock* (Munich: Fink, 1997).

[15] Korsakov, "Beschreibung," 59.

[16] Ibid., 60.

[17] Ibid.

[18] Ibid., 67.

[19] Ibid.

[20] Ibid., 68.

[21] Ibid., 61.

[22] Ibid., 60.

[23] Ibid., 61.

[24] Ibid., 60–61.

[25] Ibid., 62.

[26] Ibid., 70.

[27] Ibid., 62.

[28] Ibid., 73.

[29] Ibid., 59.

[30] See Friedrich Kittler, "Pest und Cholera. Die Geburt der Kulturwissenschaft aus dem Geiste historischer Pathologie," in *Lesbarkeit der Kultur. Literaturwissenschaften zwischen Kulturtechnik und Ethnographie*, ed. Gerhardt Neumann and Sigrid Weigel (Munich: Fink, 2000), 277–387.

[31] See Olaf Briese, *Angst in den Zeiten der Cholera*, 4 vols. (Berlin: Akademie, 2003). Briese's exhaustively researched postdoctoral dissertation presents the cultural origins of bacteriology, which he locates in the discourse around cholera, as viewed from the

perspective of "the history of science and of knowledge."

[32] Michel Foucault, *The Birth of the Clinic: An Archaeology of Medical Perception*, trans. A. M. Sheridan (New York: Vintage, 1994).

[33] Korsakov, "Beschreibung," 61.

[34] Imperial Academy of Sciences, "Urteil des Gremiums der St. Petersburger Akademie über den Antrag von S. Karsakov," in Velminski and Ernst, *Semen Karsakov*, 85.

Chapter 5

[1] Benoît Mandelbrot, *The Fractal Geometry of Nature* (New York: Freeman, 1982), 2–4.

[2] Ibid., 422–24.

[3] A. A. Markov, "Primer statisticheskogo issledovaniya nad tekstom "Evgeniya Onegina," illyustriruyuschiy svyaz' ispytaniy v tsep,'" *Izvestiya Imperatorskoy akademii nauk*, 6th ser., 7, no. 3 (1913): 153–62. For a detailed description of Markov's experiment and its consequences, see Philipp von Hilgers and Wladimir Velminski, eds., *Andrej A. Markov. Berechenbare Künste. Mathematik, Poesie, Moderne* (Zurich: Diaphanes, 2007).

[4] One indication of the importance Markov attached to his theory is provided by the statistician Alexander Chuprov (1874–1926). In a discussion of the fourth edition of *Ischisleniye veroyatnostey*, Markov's classic text on probability calculation (posthumously published in 1924), Chuprov describes the method employed by his longtime correspondent as the product of complex approaches, and predicts that Markov "will attain great prominence when he is embraced by the broad scientific audience he deserves" (Chuprov 1925, 173). See also Hilgers and Velminski, *Andrej A. Markov*, 32–39.

[5] Markov was very much involved in the organization of that celebration: see, for example, his letter to Chuprov of January 15, 1913, in Kh. O. Ondar, ed., *The Correspondence between A. A. Markov*

and A. A. Chuprov on the Theory of Probability and Mathematical Statistics, trans. Charles and Margaret Stein (New York: Springer, 1981), 65–66.

[6] N. A. Morozov, "Lingvisticheskie spektry. Sredstvo dlia otlicheniia plagiatov ot istinnykh proizvedeniy togo ili drugogo izvestnogo avtora," *Izvestiya Otdeleniya russkogo yazyka i slovesnosti Imperatorskoy Akademii nauk* 20, no. 4 (1915): 93. See also Wladimir Velminski, "Der Speck am Text. Die Entstehung der Genetik aus der Berechenbarkeit der Literatur," in Hilgers and Velminski, *Andrej A. Markov*, 101–126.

[7] N. A. Morozov, *Povesti'moyey zhizni* (Moscow: Izdatelvo Akademii nauk SSSR, 1961), 379.

[8] Morozov, "Lingvisticheskie spektry," 100.

[9] See two books by Morozov: *Die Evolution der Materie auf den Himmelskörpern. Eine theoretische Ableitung des periodischen Systems* (Dresden: T. Steinkopff, 1910) and *Die Offenbarung Johannis. Eine astronomisch-historische Untersuchung* (Stuttgart: W. Spemann, 1912).

[10] Morozov, "Lingvisticheskie spektry," 94.

[11] Ibid.

[12] Ibid., 101.

[13] Ibid., 102.

[14] Ibid., 100.

[15] Ibid., 103.

[16] Ibid., 105.

[17] Ibid., 109.

[18] A. A. Markov, "Ob odnom primeneniye statisticheskogo metoda," *Izvestiya Imperatorskoy akademii nauk*, 6th ser., 10, no. 4 (1916): 241.

[19] See for example two books by Zipf: *Selected Studies of the Principle of Relative Frequency in Language* (Cambridge, MA: Harvard University Press, 1932), and *The Psycho-Biology of Language: An Introduction to Dynamic Philology* (Cambridge, MA: Riverside

Press, 1935).

[20] See also David Crystal, ed., *The Cambridge Encyclopedia of Language* (Cambridge: Cambridge University Press, 1987), and Claudia Prün, "G. K. Zipf's Conception of Language as an Early Prototype of Synergetic Linguistics," *Journal of Quantitative Linguistics* 6, no. 1 (1999), 78–84.

[21] George Kingsley Zipf, *Human Behavior and the Principle of Least Effort: An Introduction to Human Ecology* (Cambridge, MA: Addison-Wesley, 1949), 19–55.

[22] Mandelbrot, *Fractal Geometry*, 422.

[23] Benoît Mandelbrot, "Contribution à la théorie mathématique des jeux de communication," (PhD diss., Université de Paris, 1953).

[24] Anthony Barcellos, "Benoit Mandelbrot," in *Mathematical People: Profiles and Interviews*, ed. Donald J. Albers and G. L. Alexanderson (Cambridge, MA: Birkhäuser Boston, 1984), 211.

[25] Claude E. Shannon and Warren Weaver, *The Mathematical Theory of Communication*, (Urbana: University of Illinois Press, 1998), 39.

[26] See Maarten Bullynck, "Markovketten – Variationen im Computer," in Hilgers and Velminski, *Andrej A. Markov*, 162–64.

[27] See Frieder Nake, *Ästhetik als Informationsverarbeitung. Grundlagen und Anwendungen der Informatik im Bereich ästhetischer Produktion und Kritik* (Vienna: Springer, 1974), 235.

[28] Mandelbrot, *Fractal Geometry*, 404.

Chapter 6

[1] A. K. Gastev, *Poeziya rabochego udara* (Moscow: Sovetskii pisatel', 1964), 222.

[2] The theater director Vsevolod Meyerhold, seeing the potential of this simultaneously rational/scientific and playful/poetic approach, invited Gastev and his colleagues to give lectures at the State Academy of Theater Arts. Meyerhold had developed a

new acting technique he called biomechanics, in direct reference to research then being done by Nikolai Bernstein at Gastev's institute: see N. Bernstein, *The Co-ordination and Regulation of Movements*, (Oxford: Pergamon, 1967); as well as Irina Sirotkina, "Istoriia tsentral'nogo instituta truda: Voploshcheniye utopii?" *Voprosy istorii estestvoznaniia i tekhniki* 12, no. 2 (1991): 67–72.

[3] Passages from two of Gastev's books are particularly illuminating here: *Kak nado rabotat': Prakticheskoye vvedeniye v nauku organizatsii truda* (Moscow: Ekonomika, 1966), 17–19; and *Trudovye ustanovki* (Moscow: CIT, 1973), 54–63. See also Kendall Bailes, "Alexei Gastev and the Soviet Controversy over Taylorism, 1918–24," *Soviet Studies* 29, no. 3 (July 1977): 373–94; and Wladimir Velminski, "Werkbankvision. Das Einstellen des Erfindens mit der Poesie des Hammerschlags," in *Ultravision. Zum Wissenschaftsverständnis der Avantgarde*, ed. Sabine Flach and Margarete Vöhringer (Munich: Fink, 2009), 129–46.

[4] Cf. Rolf Hellebust, "Aleksei Gastev and the Metallization of the Revolutionary Body," *Slavic Review* 56, no. 3 (Fall 1997): 500–518.

[5] Gastev, *Trudovye ustanovki*, 138–45. See also Bernstein, *Co-ordination and Regulation*, as well as Margarete Vöhringer, *Avantgarde und Psychotechnik. Wissenschaft, Kunst und Technik der Wahrnehmungsexperimente in der frühen Sowjetunion* (Göttingen: Wallstein, 2007).

[6] Gastev and Lenin met for the last time in June 1921, at which time they discussed "the CIT product"; the Council of Labor and Defense issued a decree regarding the CIT in August of that same year. Gastev, *Kak nado rabotat'*, 7. See also A. K. Gastev, "Svidanie s Leninym," in *Lenin vsegda s nami. Vospominaniya sovetskikh i zarubezhnykh pisateley*, ed. Nina I. Krutikova (Moscow: Khudozhestvennaya literatura, 1967), 402–4.

[7] Frederick Winslow Taylor, *The Principles of Scientific Management* (New York: Harper & Brothers, 1911). See also Bettina Heintz, *Die Herrschaft der Regel. Zur Grundlagengeschichte des Computers*

(Frankfurt: Campus, 1993); Angelika Ebbinghaus, *Arbeiter und Arbeitswissenschaft. Zur Entstehung der "wissenschaftlichen Betriebsführung"* (Opladen: Westdeutscher Verlag, 1984); and Karl Markus Michel and Harald Wieser, eds., "Arbeitsorganisation – Ende des Taylorismus?" special issue, *Kursbuch*, no. 43 (March 1976).

[8] V. I. Lenin, "The Immediate Tasks of the Soviet Government," trans. Clemens Dutt, in *Collected Works*, vol. 27, *February–July 1918*, ed. Robert Daglish (Moscow: Progress Publishers, 1974), 235–77. See also V. I. Lenin, *O nauchnoy organizatsii truda* (Moscow: Izdatel'stvo politicheskoy literatury, 1970).

[9] Gastev, *Poeziya rabochego udara*, 284.

[10] For further discussion of the term *preset* as used by Gastev, see Velminski, "Werkbankvision," 134–36.

[11] Gastev, *Trudovye ustanovki*, 86.

[12] Ibid., 88.

[13] Ibid., 89.

[14] Ibid.

[15] Ibid.

[16] Ibid.

[17] Ibid., 91.

[18] Ibid., 92.

[19] Ibid., 93.

[20] Ibid.

[21] Ibid.

[22] For more on Gastev's use of recording and projection equipment, see Barbara Wurm, "Gastevs Medien. Das 'Foto-Kino-Labor' des CIT," in *Laien, Lektüren, Laboratorien. Wissenschaften und Künste in Russland 1850–1960*, ed. Matthias Schwartz, Wladimir Velminski and Torben Philipp (Frankfurt: Peter Lang, 2008), 347–90.

[23] See also Bernstein, *Co-ordination and Regulation*.

[24] Gastev, *Trudovye ustanovki*, 96.

[25] Ibid., 97.

[26] Gastev, *Poeziya rabochego udara*, 177.

[27] Gastev, *Trudovye ustanovki*, 97.

[28] Ibid., 98.

[29] Ibid., 102.

[30] Ibid., 103

[31] Ibid., 104.

[32] Ibid., 105.

[33] V. I. Lenin, *State and Revolution* (New York: International Publishers, 1932), 42–44.

Chapter 7

[1] Jonathan Crary, *24/7: Late Capitalism and the Ends of Sleep* (London: Verso, 2013), 120–21.

[2] Bernard Kazhinsky, *Biologicheskaya radiosvyaz'?* (Kiev: Akademiya nauk USSR, 1962). For a broader discussion of the concept of telepathy during this era, see: Stefan Andriopoulos, "Okkulte und technische Television," in *1929. Beiträge zur Archäologie der Medien*, ed. Stefan Andriopoulos and Bernhard J. Dotzler (Frankfurt: Suhrkamp, 2002), 31–53; Wolfgang Hagen, "Der Okkultismus der Avantgarde um 1900," in *Konfigurationen. Zwischen Kunst und Medien*, ed. Sigrid Schade and Georg Christoph Tholen (Munich: Fink, 1999), 338–57; and Peter Geimer, "Telepathie," in *Science & Fiction. Über Gedankenexperimente in Wissenschaft, Philosophie und Literatur*, ed. Thomas Macho and Annette Wunschel (Frankfurt: Fischer, 2004), 287–309.

[3] Velimir Khlebnikov, "The Radio of the Future," in *Collected Works of Velimir Khlebnikov*, trans. Paul Schmidt, vol. 1, *Letters and Theoretical Writings* (Cambridge, MA: Harvard University Press, 1987), 395.

[4] Cornelius Borck, *Hirnströme. Eine Kulturgeschichte der Elektroenzephalographie* (Göttingen: Wallstein, 2005), 266.

[5] Ivan Petrovich Pavlov, "The Identity of Inhibition with Sleep and Hypnosis," *Scientific Monthly* 17, no. 6 (1923): 605
[6] Ivan Petrovich Pavlov, "Relation between Excitation and Inhibition, Delimitation between Excitation and Inhibition, Experimental Neuroses in Dogs," in *Selected Works*, trans. S. Belsky (Moscow: Foreign Languages Publishing House, 1955), 242.
[7] Robert L. Williams and Wilse B. Webb, *Sleep Therapy: A Bibliography and Commentary* (Springfield: Charles C. Thomas, 1966), 13–16.
[8] Ivan Petrovich Pavlov, *Conditioned Reflexes: An Investigation of the Physiological Activity of the Cerebral Cortex*, trans. G. V. Anrep (London: Oxford University Press, 1927), 388.
[9] F. M. Wageneder and H. Hafner, "Elektroschlaf. Eine neue Therapieform," *Der Anaesthesist* 14, no. 4 (1965): 126–29.
[10] F. M. Wageneder, St. Schuy, T. I. Kiss, and H. Scholl, "Electrosleep Therapy in the Treatment of Insomnia," in *Electrotherapeutic Sleep and Electroanesthesia. Proceedings of the First International Symposium, Graz, Austria, 12–17 September 1966*, ed. F. M. Wageneder and St. Schuy (Amsterdam: Excerpta, 1967), 124.
[11] [Pavel Gulyaev], "Biologicheskaya svyaz' deystvuyet," Antologiya tainstvennykh sluchayev, *Tekhnika-molodezhi*, December 1968, 15. See also Oliver J. Caldwell and Loren R. Graham, *Moscow in May 1963: Education and Cybernetics* (Washington, DC: U.S. Department of Health, Education, and Welfare Office of Education, 1964).
[12] [Gulyaev], "Biologicheskaya svyaz' deystvuyet," 14.
[13] Anatoly Kashpirovsky, "Seans zdorov'ya vracha-psikhoterapevta Anatoliya Mikhaylovicha Kashpirovskogo," part 1, 58:32, televised October 9, 1989, USSR Channel One, posted by Anatoly Kashpirovsky, October 9, 2015, http://www.youtube.com/watch?v=oFDMJ3KkKrg.
[14] Kashpirovsky, "Seans zdorov'ya."
[15] Alexander Belyaev, "Chelovek, kotoryy ne spit," in *Golova professora Douelya* (Moscow: ZiF, 1926).